Memories of a Tatar Childhood

Memories of a Tatar Childhood

Guzel Amalrik

Translated from the Russian by
Marc E. Heine

Hutchinson of London

Hutchinson & Co. (Publishers) Ltd
3 Fitzroy Square, London W1P 6JD

London Melbourne Sydney Auckland
Wellington Johannesburg and agencies
throughout the world

First published 1979

Set in Monotype Garamond

Printed in Great Britain by
The Anchor Press Ltd and bound by
Wm Brendon & Son Ltd
both of Tiptree, Essex

British Library CIP data
Amalrik, Guzel
Memories of a Tatar Childhood.
1. Moscow – Social life and customs
I. Title
947'.31 DK600

ISBN 0 09 139890 8

Contents

First impressions

The first impression of my awakening consciousness was of suddenly glimpsing twin girls with fairly light brown braids close beside me. They were trying to take me in their arms, and I was lying in bed wrapped up in a blanket. I cannot picture my mother, who breast-fed me daily, almost hourly. All I remember is how one of the twins pushed the other one away in an attempt to grab me. Mama was very likely out in the kitchen, and the girls had been tempted to take me in their arms. I cannot say for sure just how old they were, perhaps seven or eight. Later, when I myself was seven or eight and was by then living opposite the house in the basement of which my consciousness had been awakened, I glimpsed twin girls of about fifteen walking past the house in which I had lived before. When I saw them I remembered them being in my basement then.

The basement where I lived was very gloomy. I cannot remember it in the daylight, only at night. I remember the night and a large black room, the walls of which glimmered gloomily through the darkness. They seemed to recede, far away from me, and in the middle of the room I saw an enormous figure with long black hair and outstretched arms reaching all the way to the ceiling. It appeared to be moving towards me, and I was very frightened. I began to scream and cry. Mama woke up, came over and asked why I was crying. I went on crying and pointed my finger at the figure and said that I was afraid of this terrible lady who reached all the way to the ceiling. Mama laughed, went over to where the woman was standing and said that this was a post, and that there was a coat and shawl hanging on the post. Mama set my mind at rest, and I gradually fell asleep.

When I was four or five we moved from the basement into a house on the other side of that narrow street with its clanking, thundering trams. In sharp contrast to the dark room with its nocturnal monsters, I now see a bright, sunny, happy spot: I very clearly recall white walls and sunbeams and also, for some reason, a black rosette on the radio. There were two windows with big, deep sills where one could not merely sit, but even lie, just like on a sofa. Sometimes on summer evenings I used to lie there on my bedclothes, feeling very jealous of the other children my age, who could play outside, running about and shouting, while I couldn't walk yet; my legs were shaped like a wheel and were so deformed that the most I could do was to crawl on all fours: I suffered from rickets and did not begin to walk on my own until I was six. I watched from our second-floor window with envy and longing, running my finger along the window pane, then turned away sadly and looked back at the room. It was hazy from cigarette smoke, and I could see my papa and his three brothers. One of them I particularly liked. He had thick black hair, a dark complexion and fiery eyes which looked at me very affectionately from behind his glasses. He also had thick lips.

The brothers were speaking in Tatar and arguing about something the whole time – in a low voice, because there were neighbours on the other side of the wall. As they talked they often referred to a man whom they called in Tatar the '*kara kyut*', that is, 'black ass'. I remember quite distinctly that they strongly disapproved of this 'black ass'; from what they said it appeared that this 'black ass' was going to lead to no good. My favourite uncle said that he often listened to the 'Voice of America', but only secretly, with the sound turned down so the neighbours wouldn't hear.

'Oh, how they criticize this "black ass" in America!' uncle would exclaim, adding in a low voice that for picking up America on the radio he could be arrested, because it was illegal.

I began to feel curious and, raising myself and looking at my favourite uncle, asked, 'Papa, who is this "black ass"?' I always liked to repeat words that caught my fancy.

Uncle smiled and in a loud, surprised voice called me over

and said he would show me something. Mama helped me to get up off the window sill, and I crawled over to my uncle as quickly as I could. He sat me on his knees – and I started to sneeze from his tobacco smell. Then he took out a small package, turned it over in his hands, took something out of it and exclaimed loudly, 'See, I've brought you a bonnet as a gift!' The bonnet was a dark pink colour and very fluffy. I was terribly pleased with it. He put it on my head, and I felt very happy. I even forgot my question about the 'black ass' and America.

The brothers were great friends then, their closeness stemming from the fact that they had come to Moscow together from the country. They had fled wartime hunger, selling everything they owned for bread. In Moscow father had found a job as a loader at one of the stations: he unloaded goods wagons. I remember how, when I was four or five, he turned up unexpectedly from somewhere, wearing army boots and a greatcoat; mama was terribly pleased by his arrival. It was awfully cold, and his coat was covered in snow. He was carrying a number of gifts: there were pretty little boots for me, and red satin for a dress. I liked the boots so much that I could not fall asleep until late that night, and I kept getting up out of bed and crawling over to the wardrobe to stroke them. I also recall that he brought us some tins which he said were 'American', and a Swiss watch which I can't remember later: he probably sold it. Then father jokingly pinned a medal on my chest, but I don't know what was on the medal; I think now it must have been a medal to commemorate the 800th anniversary of Moscow. In 1947 everyone without exception received one.

My parents had a hard time adjusting to city ways. Not knowing the Russian language, culture or mode of life, they and all my relations arrived in this huge city quite unprepared for the tempo of urban life. Uprooted from their rural way of life, they found it extremely difficult to get settled in town, and they had little contact with their surroundings. From earliest childhood I recall that Russians treated Tatars with extreme animosity; I am speaking of working-class Russians – I knew no others. Maybe this was a result of their lack of education and the generally gloomy atmosphere of their difficult life. As

I recall, mama would take me outdoors from time to time and seat me on a chair, and the girls and boys would look at me and begin to laugh and shout, calling me 'Tatar' and 'bow-legged' and throwing whatever rubbish they could find at me. One of the girls came up and offered me some bread and curds, or so she said. I grabbed it greedily, because I was very hungry, but it proved to be inedible: it was a stale crust from the rubbish heap, on which a stony white mortar like slaked lime or alabaster had been piled. Apparently they liked to laugh at me.

At about this time my sister Sonya was born: I have no recollection of her before I was eight. My mama fed her copiously, and me as well: I drank her milk from a cup. It had a sweetish taste. Mama also gave milk at a donor station – she was like a dairy cow, giving two litres a day there. She was paid for it, and I was even granted free meals at state expense in a special dietary kitchen, for my rickets were the result of hunger. Later, I drank my mother's milk after the birth of the other children, too.

Our family history

I was born in the middle of the war, in 1942, in a village near Nizhny Novgorod. According to mama, there had been other children before me: three girls and twin boys, but they had all died. The twin boys, the last to be born before me, had lived to the age of three: they were very pretty, dark-eyed and fair, but they caught dysentery and died. I was the first child to survive, although I was very sickly. I was a babe in arms when my parents fled our starving village for Moscow in 1943. We lived in a basement then. I do not remember what our room was like, only that mama said that we had a cement floor. Later, I recall, mama used to talk about how she had lived before: she always compared that time, when life had been better, with her present life. She said that before collectivization they had lived well: they had had a nice house and a farm with livestock and poultry. Although in the summer time they had had to work from dawn to dusk, it had all been for themselves, and in winter they rested, and the women spun, knitted and embroidered. She sadly recalled her early years and wept bitterly. She talked about the lovely Sunday outings they used to have. All the lads and girls would get together and go off to the bazaar in carts pulled by three horses with bells. There would be more young people at the bazaar, and what couldn't you buy there? – morocco slippers, and beautiful earrings, and dresses, and the brightest shawls, and more sweets than you could count. A splendid round loaf of bread cost only two kopecks. They would choose some sweets, and their hearts would fill with joy. Meanwhile the lads in their boots were winking dashingly at the girls. The lads loved playing games; they liked to show off their strength, especially in front of the girls. These were Tatar games: for example, riding horseback – and whoever knocked someone else off his horse was declared top rider.

I loved mama dearly when she used to sit calmly and peacefully on a stool – we had no chairs – telling me stories while combing her hair. She had very long, soft black hair then, with a silken lustre to it. She used to draw her comb slowly through her hair and sometimes, pausing in the middle, think of something and then suddenly break into a Tatar song, recalling youthful memories. Then, making a long parting in her hair, she would toss it all back, and I could see tears in her eyes. I was eight or nine then. Mama also spoke with tender emotion of winter outings and games. She could remember the winters, the moonlit evenings when the girls and lads met to go sledding, and the sled would be enormous, with room for ten people. The winters were dry and cold, and mama wore only a long dress with no trousers, and a sheepskin coat – but she wasn't cold, because she was having such a good time. Huddling together, they would tear downhill with a whoop, and the sled would speed a long, long way off and crash into a pit, and with a screech they would fall head over heels on top of one another. They would climb back up with the sled and then rush downhill again with a shout of joy, into that blissful pit of still unrealized passions. When mama recounted this her face looked sly and radiant. She obviously liked recalling those blissful, carefree days. Mama said that manners and morals were pure then; they feared God and their fathers and there was no coarseness. Mama was fifteen then; I was sixteen when she told me these things.

Unfortunately, I know very little about my forefathers, and in fact I was told practically nothing about them, because my parents themselves could remember almost nothing. From what my father did tell me, I remember only that my great-grandfather was a very interesting man who had been drawn to religion, travelled to Cairo in his youth and there entered a madrasah. While in Egypt he married an Egyptian girl, so I have Arabian as well as Tatar blood in my veins. After completing the madrasah he returned home and became a mullah. Father and uncle said that he was also a religious writer and wrote many books, besides which he was a skilled orator and preached Islam to the uneducated Tatars; he also cured the sick and helped the poor, so the people loved him, thronging to him from the whole neighbourhood, and from far-away places as well, bringing him their illnesses and asking his help and blessing. In his books he wrote about what he had learned, but along came the revolution, and he was obliged to bury his books under the mosque to hide them from the revolutionaries. Shortly thereafter he died an absurd death: having eaten three hard-boiled eggs he developed a twisting of the bowel, and thus ended his glorious religious life. My grandfather, on the other hand, was a less gifted man and left nothing behind him but a son, that is to say, my father, aged seven years. My father completed only three years in a Tatar school and then left. He had had a very strict teacher in his form who always had a heavy cane at his side. As soon as he noticed that someone was not listening, he would raise his cane and beat him very violently. Unable to bear such strictness, father left school, going out to work from his earliest years. Life was very difficult at the time and there was no bread, but to make up for it the workers and peasants were in power.

In 1936 or 1937 father was married off – without even being asked whether he wanted to be or not – to my mother, a girl of seventeen, whom he had seen only once before. She wasn't asked either, and she didn't even know him. That was how they were married. According to her own account, as a young girl mama had loved a red-haired lad who died shortly after her marriage, apparently of tuberculosis. Once she was married children began to appear, and to die just as quickly. With my appearance my parents began to think of leaving their starving village for town, and a year later we moved to Moscow. Father had been declared unfit for military service: he had bad vision and was invalided out. I remember how he liked to use his official disability to buy flour; at the time it was very difficult to get flour, and when it arrived large numbers of people would collect, a thousand or so. They had their number in the queue written on their palms with indelible pencil, and if it turned out that the same number occurred twice, they threw the extra person out of the queue. Approaching the queue, my father would immediately alter his gait, becoming lame in one leg.

He then went up to the shop girl with his money, while the queue naturally yelled at him, but waving his invalid card from a distance, he would shout, 'I'm an invalid of the Patriotic War; I have the right to be served out of turn!' And they would give him the set ration – I can no longer remember how much it was – three or four kilos, I think.

When I was six, a woman turned up in our house quite unexpectedly and began living with us. She had a very sad, very beautiful face and was fairly short and thin, with black hair. She often played and talked with me, and I loved her because of this. I liked to look at her and felt a strange tenderness towards her: perhaps it was her beauty which produced such a profound effect. I cannot remember her name, but the beautiful woman is associated in my mind with a yellow wooden floor, scrubbed spotless (she washed it frequently and made easy going of it), a hot stove, gleams of light and a picture of a mosque on a wall. But later the beautiful woman disappeared, going away somewhere. Afterwards mama told me that the woman had been the fiancée of my uncle on the maternal side, and that she had waited for him all through the war, and even later, but all the same she had waited in vain. News arrived that he had disappeared without a trace, and that was why he hadn't come back. Mama said that when war began he had not wanted to fight, either out of cowardice or because he did not like killing, and he had decided to hide under the floor of the house. They brought him food, but he did not succeed in staying hidden for long, being given away by his own neighbours, who used to come to see him. Officers arrived, dragged him away and put him in a punishment battalion. Maybe he was shot by his own people, or maybe he was killed by a German bullet.

Grandmother

My grandmother on my father's side was paralysed in old age and was always bed-ridden, only getting out of bed with someone's help when she had to relieve herself. Grandmother was unbelievably mean. I remember how once the two of us were sitting together at home, and I was combing my hair furiously with a fine-tooth comb. The whole time I was twitching nervously from the lice which were furrowing my head and body. I spread out some white paper on a stool and began combing the lice on to it. There were more than I could count. I cruelly crushed them on the paper with my thumbnail, and this made a 'crack-crack' sound, which made my body go cold and I got the shivers. Suddenly the bed began to creak and my old grandmother's voice echoed the cracking sound, like a rusty old trough, which very much frightened me. 'What?' cried grandmother. 'Are you eating sugar without permission?!' She had mistaken the crackling of the lice being squashed for the crackling of sugar and even tried to raise her body, despite the fact that she was paralysed. I was very frightened of her, so I took the stool with the paper, held it up to the bed and showed her what I had been doing. But she did not really believe me and went on muttering abuse, threatening to tell my father and mama.

My grandmother was very fond of teaching me prayers, and she often read to me from the Koran. I can remember little of what she read and said to me, but certain prayers remain in my memory, and even now I sometimes say them to myself, quite meekly and sincerely. But then, when I listened to her Arabic prayers and readings, it was solely out of respect and fear that she would scream at me. I even found it boring. She reckoned that even though I understood nothing at the time, later on I would remember it all and understand. What was important was that I should be imbued with a religious spirit.

All in all, I didn't like my grandmother very much. Old and malicious, she lay paralysed throughout the whole of my childhood, and like all sick persons she demanded excessive attention, which it was impossible to give in our terrible conditions. I recall one episode connected with her malice. Once, when I was about seven, grandmother and I were alone, father and mother being at work. I was asleep, but suddenly I heard an object crash against my bed and loud knocking at the door. It turned out that my father had come home from work and had been knocking at the door for some time. I had been sleeping very soundly and had heard nothing, so grandmother had taken a tray that had been lying beside her and threw it at me, but fortunately it had not hit me, though it fell close by, striking the bed with a crash and a clang. At this point I woke up and opened the door for father.

There was a bucket for grandmother right in our room, and she used to relieve herself in it. When mama and papa were at work, I used to try to help her to get up, but she was too heavy for me, and I had difficulty in helping her to raise her emaciated body. Once she accidentally kicked the bucket over with her paralysed leg, and almost the entire contents spilled on to the floor and trickled across the room. The stench was unbearable. I had the difficult task of cleaning it up all by myself, and as I did it I began to weep from the awful stench, and out of a feeling of bitterness that although I was small, it was I who had to clean it up. At that moment our neighbour, Aunt Shura, dropped in by chance to ask my mother something. She had a brick-shaped loaf of white bread in her hands and I looked at it greedily. Noticing my hungry stare, Aunt Shura broke off a big hunk and I grabbed it without saying a word, quickly devouring the spongy bread. It was so soft and tasty – it may have seemed so because I was so hungry at the time – and I'm sure I shan't find the like of it now. As I greedily ate the bread, it smelled very strongly of shit. The poorly scrubbed room must have smelled of it, or else the smell came from my dirty hands, but for a long time afterwards the taste of bread was associated in my mind with the smell of shit. I never managed to eat my fill of bread. I remember there was a bakery not far from our house, and I used to peer greedily through the bakery window as the bakers in their white shirts and trousers worked surrounded by heat and delicious smells. I had made up my mind to ask for a roll whenever they noticed me through the window. Sometimes they gave me one, and I would thank the baker joyfully and munch on the delicious roll.

When I was eight or nine, I was walking around outside and for some reason mama called me. I went over to her, but she was silent and said nothing. I asked her why she had called me, but all she said was, 'Come along', and she led me into our room. I thought that perhaps I had done something wrong in the room, and that she was going to punish me. I entered the room, which was unusually silent, and saw my grandmother lying motionless on the floor. Her face was sharp and chiselled, the colour of saffron. Mama stood there saying nothing, as before. Then she took me by the shoulders and said softly, 'Grandmother is dead.' I was surprised and asked what she meant by 'dead'. I wanted to go over to grandmother and wake her up, but mama grabbed me. I again asked what she meant by 'dead'. Mama said that while I was out walking and she was doing the laundry, grandmother took a turn for the worse and kept asking for something to drink. Then she began to suffocate, and she asked to be placed on the floor. Mama did as grandmother requested, and once on the floor she sighed deeply and quietly passed away. Mama covered her face with a large white handkerchief and sent me outside. Father was at work at the time.

A day or two later – I do not remember exactly – our relations arrived, our grandmother's children, to say farewell to her. She was lying dressed and wrapped up in a white sheet, in a deep box which father himself had knocked together out of planks. Everyone began to kiss grandmother. When my turn came, I went up to the box, but I couldn't reach her face, so someone lifted me up and bent me down. I did not want to kiss her, but everyone was watching me so I was forced to kiss her cold cheeks. Then they took her away. The box appeared very heavy – four or five men carried it. When they took it through the courtyard, almost all the tenants in the house gathered out of curiosity to watch the spectacle. After everyone had left for the cemetery, some women asked me why they were burying her in a box. Were they short of money, or was that the custom? I simply said I didn't know, but I had a lump in my throat and was ready to cry. I left the women quickly and ran off to play, and to this day I do not know why they buried her in a box. Evidently they simply did not have the money, but all the same my parents invited a great number of guests to her funeral feast. I remember that mama made Tatar pilau, with raisins: this is a special pilau which they eat at funeral feasts.

So grandmother died, and it was even strange not to hear her prayers and readings from the Koran; but, frankly, I felt better without her. I no longer felt her eye always on me; I didn't have to hear her shrill, old woman's cry; I didn't have to clean up after her from time to time.

Of my maternal grandmother I have little recollection. Possibly, she only came to Moscow to visit my mama once. This is how I remember her: she seemed to be sitting on a chair, but for some reason the chair was standing on the bed, and she was very tall and stately, with long black hair without so much as a single grey strand. It was raven-black. I remember that her face was very beautiful and fair, with dark blue eyes; a large bunch of ring-shaped crackers lay at her feet. That's all; I can't remember anything more.

The birth of my brother

When I was five, my brother Mansur was born. All I remember of his birth is one episode. One day the *babai* arrived with a razor in his hand. First he began to mumble some prayers; then, closing his eyes, he intoned them in a thin, shrill voice. Mama held my brother's little body, and the *babai* began his nasty work. I did not understand what was going on, but I felt that the *babai* was doing something bad. The *babai* ordered mama to send me outside, but I did not go outside. Instead, I lurked by the door, listening. I was quiet at first. Then my brother started to scream and cry, and I began to feel very sorry for him. I thought: what are they doing to him? I wanted to come in, but the door turned out to be hooked shut. Feeling helpless, I began to weep in the corridor and pound on the door. When they had finished humiliating my brother, they let me back in and then I saw him in a kind of trough, tired and covered in tears; and then they lifted him out of the trough and placed him in his cot, and mama bound his legs together and elevated him a bit by means of a rope attached to a nail in the wall. After praying some more the *babai* accepted some money from mother and, taking a bite to eat, left us.

Afterwards mama told me that this was a kind of rite, and that they circumcise all boys to join them to God, like Russian christening, only the Russians christen by dipping the infant in water. I don't remember exactly where I heard this, whether it was from mother or the *babai* who often visited us on Fridays to read prayers, but apparently the Muslim rite is more correct than the Orthodox one. But I don't know why it is more correct; it seems to me that it is one and the same thing.

Illnesses, delirium

One day I decided to go outdoors on my own, without anybody's help. I was then already about six, perhaps. It was a hot summer, and I longed to go outside. This was a great adventure for me, crawling on all fours out of the room and into the lengthening corridor. The corridor was made of cement and there were five doors on the left and five on the right: there was living accommodation on the right, and on the left, opposite each room, a private storage room. Passing down this long, cold corridor, I came out on to a landing lit up by a window, and then went down an endless staircase from the second floor. I remember that this was an interminable journey for me, but at last I reached the outside. I began playing in the sand, but suddenly I could hear shouts: 'Rozka, you've lost something!' I glanced round, and there were two women sitting and talking about how something was dropping out of my shorts. Frightened, I looked round and saw huge worms some ten centimetres long crawling out of me. I was terribly frightened and quickly crawled far away from them. Near by, the yard-keeper happened to be sweeping the yard. He saw my worms and, with a cry of surprise, shovelled them up, while the women, who were sitting idly on a bench shelling sunflower seeds, continued their discussion just as loudly as before. I felt they were criticizing me and making fun of me. I remember how they kept on repeating, 'That's a Tatar for you!'

Those worms gave me no rest until I was fifteen; I suffered from them the whole time. I was sick every day, and drank water endlessly. They came right up to my throat and greedily sucked in the water. Whatever I ate found its way to those damned worms, and they became more and more brazen, and fatter and fatter. They would not let me sleep, and I would not let my parents sleep. I asked them to stand a small table at the head of my bed in place of a pillow, and I passed my nights sitting up with my head propped against the table, a jar of water beside me. My face was saffron-coloured from the worms, and my body gradually became eaten up by them. I was so skinny that you could always count the ribs on my sides. My mama got a so-called remedy somewhere and treated me with it, but it hardly helped. I couldn't sleep at night and always felt sick, just as before. At last, after long sufferings, mama decided to take me to a doctor, who prescribed some kind of bitter seed, called santonica. I felt a little better afterwards, but even so I was always tense, waiting each night for those life-suckers to crawl right up to my throat. The worms reduced me to such a point that I began to be delirious at night, walking about the room with my hallucinations and frightening my parents. By the age of six or seven I had started to recover from rickets and began to walk.

I remember how one night I woke up delirious, muttering something, went over to the table and began rummaging about. I regained consciousness for a moment but then fell back into a deep sleep. Standing up in my sleep, I remembered what I was looking for: I was looking for a knife, and I started rummaging about on the table again in search of a knife. The next moment I returned to reality again and forgot why I was there, then muttered something to myself, recalling what had only just slipped away from me. I woke up again to find myself standing by the table, and suddenly a terrible whisper jolted me: 'What are you looking for?' It was mama, who had been woken up by my mutterings and was frightened by what I had been doing. I was standing bent over the table, my hand outstretched, searching for something. She repeated her question, but I couldn't understand her: the question wasn't getting through to me. She repeated it a second time – and at last I understood what she was asking. I made every effort to recall what I was looking for. The word was dangling on the tip of my tongue, and I even had the beginning of it, but I had difficulty recalling the whole thing and saying it straight away. Then suddenly my head began to clear, and I uttered the word: 'kn-i-i-ife, kn-i-i-ife', though I myself was surprised that I should all of a sudden need a knife. Mama got up, put me to bed, and covered me up with a blanket.

Another time, too, I recall, I got up in delirium and crawled under my bed to look for galoshes which in reality I didn't have. I rummaged under the bed in vain, again forgetting what I was looking for, falling back to sleep, into a kind of delirium. Once again mama was woken up by my mutterings, just like the other time, and she put me back to bed. I cannot say whether my eyes were open or not, but I remember distinctly how confidently I went over to the table, despite the fact that there was a divan bed standing in my way. Every piece of furniture was imprinted on my brain as if it had been photographed, and I could see them round me as though my movements were being guided by some sort of cerebral photosignal apparatus. Mama told me afterwards that while I was walking in my sleep my eyes were closed. Once mama caught me in the corridor. How many movements can one make in one's sleep – movements more automatically consecutive, brief and exact than in real life? I did everything with such dexterity: first I got up, then I went into the kitchen, took the big hook off the door, turned the key and went out. I recall that in real life I had great difficulty in removing this hook. It all seems a mystery to me now. To all appearances this is somnambulism, but I no longer sleep-walk now, though I do sometimes talk in my sleep.

On the whole, these continual illnesses – rickets, worms, pneumonia and tonsillitis, not forgetting influenza – turned me into a bundle of nerves. During my sleepless nights I liked to let my imagination wander: that was my favourite pastime. The most exciting and at the same time most frightening thing was the approach of school. I imagined my future teacher – for some reason she was young, beautiful and slender – and I thought about how I was going to like her and earn nothing but fives. I already understood that a mark of five was something good, but I still didn't know how one earned a five, or for that matter a two. These numbers sounded like some sort of abstraction to me, but I had heard from grown-ups that it was good to get nothing but fives; and when someone asked me what I was going to get, I would say uncertainly that I was going to get fives.

Beggars

Our room was small – only fourteen square metres – with two small windows. Between the two windows, next to the wall, stood a large, very high, almost patriarchal table, which I could sit at only if I was perched on the window sill and thus able to compete with tall, grown-up people. To the right of one of the windows, next to the wall, stood an old brown commode, and here, too, was my parents' bed. To the left of the other window, next to the wall, stood my grandmother's bed, and also my bed, where I slept with my little brother. Along the wall near my bed there was a large, green metal trunk, which served as a wardrobe. All different kinds of clothes were piled in the trunk. At night a divan bed was placed in the middle of the room; my younger sister Sonya slept here. On the wall above grandmother's bed there was a glass-framed picture of a mosque; under the mosque there was part of a prayer, written in Arabic letters. Opposite the windows, next to the wall, stood a large Dutch stove; why it was called Dutch, I don't know. Lots of people used to have such stoves. In the corner behind the stove there was a door on to the communal corridor, which led to the laundry. On the corridor opposite each room there was a storeroom of six to eight square metres. People usually kept firewood in these storerooms: there were no gas stoves yet, and in winter people cooked food on the stove, while in summer they used an oil stove. The oil stove left a strong smell of kerosene in the room, and the ceiling and walls used to get covered in soot.

When I was eight or nine, father was working as a stoker and yard-keeper. One day strange, ragged-looking people unexpectedly arrived at our place. It was obvious that they were from the country. There were perhaps four of them, all men. They asked to spend the night with us. My parents let them in, regardless of the fact that it was very crowded just by ourselves. The men were fairly young, thirty-five to forty years old, and three of them were wearing army greatcoats and shabby boots; and when they got ready for bed and took off their boots, there was the most unbearable smell of sweat. In referring to this mama always said that Russians smelled of pig.

When they came in and asked to spend the night, they said that they were all from the country, and were burned out and suffering. Their homes had been burned down, and they had come to Moscow to find work. They said they often spent the night at the railway station, but now they had decided to try to find lodgings with someone at a modest rent, namely, a rouble per person per night – a rouble was then equal to ten kopecks today. They settled down on the floor, there being no other place for them. They came the following evening as well, and in the morning they left some money and went off somewhere – we didn't know where. Once I woke up very early – my parents were still sleeping – and I saw one of them counting his money – there was a lot of it – and then he hid it somewhere. The following day I saw the same thing once again: they had all been awake for some time and were whispering and counting their money. For some reason I immediately thought how much they resembled thieves. When they came back in the evening from no one knew where, they would take out their greasy, newspaper-wrapped packages of pork, which they ate with black bread. Sometimes they drank vodka and invited father to join them. Gradually our fire victims began to feel at home with us. They discussed politics with father, one of them arguing with particular fervour. He wore an army field-shirt with some sort of shoulder straps, and he had various decorations on his chest. He considered himself a very cultured man and said that during the war he had been a battalion commander. When he said that sort of thing I always felt he was lying: I could see it in his eyes. He used to boast all the time, but once he told the truth about himself and his comrades. They had not been burned out at all; they had invented that to arouse pity and thereby get money. At their collective farm they hadn't been paid a thing;

they had been unable to feed their families, and the state took high taxes, so they ran away from the farm. And this was how they supported themselves and helped their families: they went from house to house where the higher ranks, the colonels and generals, lived and tried their best to look proud and worthy as they modestly depicted their grievous plight, mentioning that several houses had been burned down, and they had neither homes nor money. They were so good at moving people to pity that the generals and colonels often gave them rather impressive sums.

Sometimes these men would bring along yet another such 'fire victim' to spend the night in our place. My parents had already begun to worry about the neighbours becoming suspicious. After all, we were being visited by a crowd of suspicious-looking people, half-ragged 'professional beggars'. Mama hardly knew where to put them, since by then there wasn't even a scrap of free floor space; everything was covered by their greatcoats. At night it was impossible to get to the lavatory, and one had to step over them or even right on them. Altogether there were eleven or twelve of us in the room, and there was no space for anyone to breathe. My parents resented sheltering them, but the money they gave us outweighed the overcrowding, so they put up with it.

One day one of the youngest, named Petya – he was handsome in a country sort of way, curly-headed, big-eyed and toothy – brought with him a beautiful young girl with dark eyes, dark brows and dark plaits adorning her head. She was short but strongly built, and spoke with a cooing Ukrainian accent. She turned out to be his bride. He asked if my parents could take her in for a short while. My parents' patience gave out and they said sternly that this was the last night they would lodge them. The next morning they all went off, leaving their doss money, and in the evening only Petya and his young beauty returned. He said he was getting a job in town and then, perhaps, he would receive a place in a hostel. My parents let them stay, feeling sorry for them, or perhaps just because of the money. They stayed a few nights and then disappeared, and none of the 'fire victims' returned. A year or two later Petya stopped by again, wearing a new coat which he had bought with the money he had earned. He had got himself a job as a chauffeur and was living in a hostel. He informed us that his wife had given him a child, but as for the others he knew nothing, nor did he know whether they were still going around pretending to be fire victims.

Dreams, music, the mountain

Most of the memories I have of myself are of the night time, these being linked not only with the worms and other illnesses that tormented me, but also with my reveries and fantasies. Perhaps the latter, too, were to some degree an illness. At night our room assumed a fantastic character. In the dim light of the house next door, shadows and objects hanging on nails in the walls appeared as fairy-tale shapes to me. One shape – a terrible monster – came down off the walls into one of my dreams. I dreamt that I was standing, quite tiny, before this hairy monster in a state of vague fear and alarm. It frightened me and at the same time attracted and excited me. It took me by its hands, which were like trees, thick and shaggy. I tried to tear myself out of its arms and began to scream, and the monster said, 'You will be my wife!' I tried to tear myself away again, and screamed, 'Mama! Mama!' I was afraid of it. At this point I woke up. Mama was standing by my bed, very frightened and praying aloud. Then she said that it was obvious that I had not said my prayers before going to bed and so I was having bad dreams.

'Mama,' I said, 'I saw a terrible monster in my dream.'

To which she replied, 'It's a devil that's keeping you awake. Turn over on your right side and say: *Auze billyagi imnya shaitanne, bismillya irrakhmyan irradjim!*' I had no more bad dreams that night.

I often had dreams in which I was flying overland, over the sea, over cities, over a precipice, sometimes in darkness. I also had dreams in which an enormous big-eyed bus named Churchill was chasing me. It pursued me tirelessly, up hill and down dale, but then I saw in the distance a narrow blue strip of river, and I ran away from the terrible bus to the blue strip and stood on it, and then the bus couldn't catch me. At this point I would wake up. Morning had long ago spread across the room, and the loudspeaker was repeating over and over again the names of a certain Churchill and Stalin. Our radio always starts at six in the morning. A chorus breaks into the Soviet national anthem and the radio goes on talking, singing and yelling without a break until evening. I remember that they repeated Stalin's name the whole time, but I attached no meaning to this, as I didn't know who this 'Stalin' was. But I gradually recalled previous conversations about the 'black ass' and began to guess who he was. I started to listen to what they said on the radio. I recall that they always repeated 'our great leader and teacher . . .' At the time I didn't understand a thing.

I listened to music on the radio with particular interest and passion. Sometimes the radio was difficult to hear, and I would take the black megaphone off the wall and hold it to my ear, twisting it around to make it louder, and although this produced no results, I went on listening to it anyway. I remember how very much I liked Aginski's polonaise, which sounded very smooth, expansive and sad, like something irrevocably lost. I still like it: it is now linked in my mind with Andrzej Wajda's film *Ashes and Diamonds*. Then came Tchaikovsky with his Russian melodies. To me his music was like the small china figure of a ballerina which a friend of mine had given me, and which stood on the old commode in our room. It seemed forever frozen, but beautiful and for some reason quickly boring, as though I had forced myself to eat a lot of cream toffees. Next came some music by Mozart. Oh, that was divine music – the sounds made me feel as if I was taking wing that very moment, and that my body was experiencing unearthly bliss. I trembled in ecstasy; my heart danced in time with the spontaneously joyful music, and I simultaneously felt an indescribable languor.

After listening to music, I could never fall asleep in the evening, undoubtedly because of the impressions which the music had left. I would lie on my back, preventing the others from sleeping by my questions and chatter. I repeated my mother's prayers mockingly, and then she would tell me to go to sleep, and silence ensued. The last window of the house next door went dark, leaving only the moon and me, lying there with my eyes open. In the house everything was asleep; I, too, wanted to fall asleep, but in vain. I would lie like that for a long time, until the moon reached my bed from the east, and I gently and imperceptibly fell asleep. But soon I unexpectedly woke up and I felt that I hadn't slept at all. I had been woken up by my parents' loud and lively talking. I could not have been more surprised, as they had told me to go to sleep, but they themselves were not sleeping. I felt that their behaviour was unusual, so I decided to observe them silently, giving no indication that I wasn't sleeping. For some reason mama was laughing, and her laughter seemed rather strange and alien, and even unpleasant to me. Then a sonorous slap against something soft resounded in the air, and there was mama's idiotic laughter again. Then they began whispering about something, and I could make out the word 'Stop' whispered by mama. 'This is very strange: maybe papa is beating her. But for some reason she isn't crying. Papa is not a nice man. He beats me, too, with his army belt, and he always manages to hit me with the end of his big brass buckle.'

Here I imperceptibly dozed off, and when I woke up again, I suddenly heard such noise and creaking that it would be difficult to describe in words all the clicking and screaming and whispering. These sounds filled the room, and everything was buzzing and whistling. Was it something rustling, or was it the wind whistling and howling? The bed screeched mournfully and seemed almost to be begging for help. I looked in the direction of the bed and saw something quite strange: there was a high mountain on the bed, rising almost to the ceiling. It rose and sank, emitting volcanic sounds. This shook me: I felt as if I had been struck by lightning. I began to stare even more fixedly in that direction, into the darkness. I tried hard to recognize my parents, perhaps, in this mountain, but it was impossible to discern anything resembling my parents. My heart was pounding loudly enough to fill the whole room in its struggle to burst out of me. I began to cough loudly, and everything in the room went quiet; but a few minutes later I could hear gentle whispering. I dared to look there again, and I could see that there was no mountain now; there was just that vague whispering. I had frightened myself by my deliberate coughing and now tried to lie quietly and not even to breathe. I closed my eyes tightly in fear, and suddenly I could hear gently trembling breathing very near my ear, and I could feel its warmth on my face. I guessed that it was mama. My heart was already on the floor, or so it seemed, and it leapt and trembled out of nervousness and fear. I squeezed my eyelids together even more strongly, and for a moment mama and I were breathing together in the same tense expectation. My eyelashes quivered, and I could even smell her face: it smelled of milk and of something else which was unrecognizable to me. I wanted her to go away; I was certain I wouldn't be able to maintain such deception and pretence on my part. Her breathing unexpectedly moved off, and I could hear a whisper: 'She's sleeping. . . .' My heart went peaceful again. I decided to cover myself up quietly with the blanket. A corner of it was slightly torn and this provided me with a safe observation point.

The mountain did not reappear, though I waited for it to do so with trembling emotion. I wanted to see it again to unravel this puzzle. I began to get bored waiting. I was sleeping with my younger brother, and for the first time I began to look at him strangely, and an unusual interest in him began to manifest itself. He was sleeping soundly, with his tiny little legs spread out. I wanted to do what I thought my parents had been doing; I wanted to make another mountain. I was interested to see what they might have been doing under the blanket. I crawled deeper under the blanket and found myself beside his legs. For some reason I touched a strange place which I had not noticed previously, and to which I had attached no significance; I felt certain shapes in my fingers quite different to my own. I did not understand what my parents had been doing, but I felt instinctively that there was some kind of link between the 'mountain' and what I had discovered on my brother, and I felt an incomprehensible interest in and attraction to him. But I also felt the tenderness of an elder sister for him: he was two, and I was seven. Yet I felt nothing pleasant, such as I thought my parents must have felt, and it seemed to me that I was doing something bad and improper. My brother stirred and turned on his side. I thought what a bad girl I was: if mama and papa found out about this, papa would beat me severely with his belt.

Under the blanket I had not understood what my parents had been doing, or how, but I knew that they, too, had been doing something bad, which I still didn't understand. Later, the next day, I felt a strange feeling towards them, especially towards mama, because mama was still expecting a child and was therefore at home all the time. I felt that for some reason she was quite a different person in the mornings than she was at night, and it seemed to me that she was treating me rather deceitfully, smiling oddly: it was as if there was a strange lady at our place. I felt that I was very clever: 'You don't know me, but I know you; I know everything about you; I know that you are bad and have unclean eyes.' I felt hostility and suspicion towards them. I think mama even sensed that something was wrong with me, and she often glanced at me on the sly. I didn't want to talk to mama and I looked at them both sullenly, imagining them that night, and whenever I thought of this I hated them. With each new day I looked more and more closely at mama and disliked her more and more. On the whole, I had never liked father: he did not know how to talk or play with me, and he never kissed me – in any case, I do not recall that he ever did. He beat me frequently, pouncing on me like a rabid tiger. As a result I feared and disliked him. Welts from his belt remain on my buttocks to the present day as a souvenir of childhood.

One day the stove in our room was broken up and a partition built in its place. Gas had been installed in the house, and the stove had become unnecessary. The partition extended as far as the middle of the room, and it would have been possible to stand my bed there, but I asked mama to place the head of my bed in the middle of the room, rather than against the wall. Somehow it was too dark and lonely against the wall, since the light from the house next door did not penetrate that far, but even more important, I would not be able to see my parents' bed. My interest in these nocturnal scenes reached such proportions that I would creep out from behind my partition and stand squeezed against the wall, peeping out warily, and highly excited. In my fear I used to think that the merest squeaking of the bed meant that someone was getting out of it, and I would lie down again quietly on my own bed, with palpitating heart. My curiosity gradually grew so keen that I began to derive a kind of pleasure from observing my parents, as I lurked, slyly and evilly, like a small animal. I think it was perhaps because I so spoilt their youth that they did not love me. Later on, I quite consciously tried to disturb them. As soon as I sensed that the moment was approaching when this very interesting thing was about to begin, I would get up ostentatiously and go into the kitchen, or cough loudly on purpose, taking pleasure in the fact that everything suddenly went dead quiet. At last mama would ask me in a bad temper why I was getting up so often and going into the kitchen, and why wasn't I sleeping? 'But I don't want to go to sleep: the worms are bothering me,' I would say slyly, though this was actually the truth, because the worms always bothered me, and that is why my feelings were so strained. I was very nervous and malicious because of all these illnesses, and even I realized that I was a bad girl.

Once, when I was perhaps fourteen, mama told me that I would not be going to school that day, but would be taking her to hospital. (They wouldn't let papa off work that day.) To be honest I didn't very much want to go with mama, but I wanted to go to school even less. I was silent the whole way there. We went by bus, then we went by tram, and I said nothing the whole way. When we reached the hospital, I told her, 'Mama, you've got no backbone, and I hate father. You're weak-willed, and I know all about you. I'll never be like you – I'll never be a weakling! If I were you, I'd kick him out. We can live without him. I'll help you with everything, and I'll be going to work soon. I'll help you to sell apples, cucumbers and tomatoes.'

I had already begun to guess why she was going to hospital. I still didn't entirely understand, but I connected it with my nocturnal observations.

Mama replied with a sad face (her face was physically exhausted – I suddenly noticed this), 'My little daughter, you understand nothing yet. You're growing up to be a big girl now, and like me you'll get married and learn what is expected of you as a woman. Then you'll think of me. Honestly, I don't in the least want it to be like this.'

I heard her out, and for some reason I began to feel a bit

sorry for her, maybe because she was so weak-willed. I replied merely that I would never marry, and with these words we entered the hospital waiting room. We kissed rather coldly, and I went off home with a bundle of mama's things in my arms. Of course I realize now that I was unfair to her, but mama was not entirely frank with me either.

The more I observed my parents, the stronger grew my interest in my brother. We children were often left alone at home when our parents went off to work in the morning. I remember when I was eleven, we were playing together, romping about on the bed – my sister Sonya, my brother Mansur (he was six), my younger sister Galya and I. We split into two groups – Mansur was in my group and Galya in Sonya's – and began throwing pillows, and feathers flew in all directions. The game was simple: whichever group captured all the pillows won. Mansur and I captured all their pillows, but the game began to bore us, and we decided to have a rest. I accidentally touched my brother, and I liked that. I wanted to touch his buttocks with my hands again: it was so exciting and happened so unnoticeably – it was all like a continuation of our game. Finally I wanted to do what my parents did, but by then I was beginning to feel ashamed. Galya and Sonya were looking at me strangely, as though they had begun to understand something. I suddenly thought that they might remember this as adults, or maybe I was afraid that somehow they would tell our parents, so I stopped my game, promising myself that this would never happen again. Galya, although only three, always watched me too intently, as a result of which I took a dislike to her.

Although I in fact realized that what I was doing was bad, I still went back to it, even though I was moved to another bed away from my brother. Now I slept with my sister Sonya and my attraction was transferred to her. We used to play a game of horse and rider, in which I was the horse, and my sister Sonya the rider. I would lie on the bed, placing her on my stomach. She would jump high up, towards the ceiling. She liked my taking her for a ride like this, and it felt very pleasant and exciting to me.

It is interesting that the sense of burning jealousy linked with hatred which I felt towards my parents when they made love at night I also extended to other loving couples whom I met on the streets. I liked to observe them secretly, feeling both jealousy and hatred; unconsciously, I also felt envy. These feelings abated by the age of fifteen, when I fell in love for the first time, but to some extent I still feel jealous of every loving couple.

Our yard

I want to talk about our yard, where I spent a lot of time until I was sixteen. Our house, in which I lived from the age of three, had been build in 1830 by a landowner named Volkov. The building contained his laundry and bath-house, and his servants also lived there. Later there weren't any more landowners, and when the Soviet regime arrived, they turned the laundry and other outbuildings into dwellings and installed people in them, while the yard became overgrown with grass taller than a man. I was told that during the New Economic Policy bandits hid there, and it also provided a cover for prostitutes. On the whole, the lodgers were newcomers like ourselves, only we arrived later. They all came from various villages and small provincial towns.

It was a large yard and on all four sides there were long benches where, I remember, women always used to sit and stare to see who was visiting whom, giving careful consideration to who was wearing what, and what the purpose of their visit was. This was always accompanied by the cracking of sunflower seeds. Not even children escaped their gaze. For the most part these women were traders in whatever came their way: fruit or vegetables. After work, some of them would organize *songfests*, and they would yell out their national songs in shrill voices. At one end of the yard there stood a large table for playing cards, lotto and dominoes. On summer evenings young people would gather to play the accordion and sing songs – most often 'The Cranes' by Petr Leshchenko, though they also sang 'Near the town of Gorky, where the dawns are bright' and other songs. The accordion was played by the only musician in the entire building: a young Chinese. Perhaps his parents had worked in the laundry during the years of the New Economic Policy, but I never saw them. The Chinese had a good ear and sang very well, so everyone loved listening to him. He was handsome, unusually tall for a Chinese, and very slender, with regular features and obviously Chinese eyes, with slightly swollen eyelids. Later he married a beautiful light-haired woman. The people in the house were very friendly to the Chinese, and he himself behaved just like a Russian amongst Russians. He spoke without an accent, since he had been born in Moscow. People treated him just like a Russian.

I loved watching the young couples who lived above us on the third floor. Their names were unusual for our building. They often quarrelled, and their dramatic cries – 'Alfred!' or 'Tamara!' – could be heard endlessly.

Slapping Alfred's face, Tamara would shout, 'I'm going to leave you, Alfred!'

She would run off, and he would shout after her, 'Come back, Tamara!' She would go on running and calling for help, threatening him with the militia, and he would shout at her, 'Bitch! Prostitute!', shaking his fists and grabbing her by the throat.

Curious heads popped out of every window. They both seemed very beautiful to me: he was a tall, lean brunette; she, a blonde, with curly hair and a slim figure. Despite the fact that they often quarrelled and fought, I think they loved each other. Such dramatic scenes excited me, and I even slightly envied the way Alfred treated Tamara. I, too, wanted someone to run after me, shouting, 'Come back, Guzel!'

For some reason everyone in the building called me Roza, although at home I was called by another name, a Tatar, not a Russian one. I still have no idea who christened me with a Russian name; my Tatar name, Guzel, means 'beautiful'. Earlier on, I had been totally unaware what my name meant and did not know that it might be beautiful. On the contrary, I was even ashamed of the name. Usually Tatar names end in a vowel, whereas mine ends in a soft consonant. Consequently, I felt that it was too long and fluffy, so I had no difficulty in accepting a Russian name. My Tatar name had been given to me by my paternal grandmother. I was also nicknamed 'kilka' (sprat). When I was five, during a time of scarcity one of my playmates gave me a dried-up sprat from the rubbish heap. I took it eagerly and ate it, and the boys and girls laughed. This unpleasant nickname stayed with me from then on. The word is similar to the Tatar '*kil*', which means 'come'. '*Kilka, kil menda!*' – 'Sprat, come here!' The Russians pronounce 'menda' with two a's, and then you get a dirty word.

My neighbour Slavka, who was lame, particularly liked to tease me – not out of malice, but because everyone teased me. He was rather friendly to me; perhaps our deformities united us: I was bandy-legged and he was lame. He also teased me by calling me 'Tatal' (he couldn't pronounce his r's), while I called him 'lame rouble'. Everyone called him that – I don't know why. Maybe he begged roubles outside the cinema. Children often do this to get into the cinema if their parents haven't given them any money.

I remember once hearing the interesting words (or so they seemed to me): 'criticism – self-criticism'. I ran out into the yard with this word which had so terribly caught my fancy, and, seeing lame Slavka, I stuck out my tongue and said, 'Hey, rouble: criticism – self-criticism, criticism – self-criticism!' I ran round him and asked, 'Do you know this word?'

But he began to snap at me, badgering me to say what kind of word it was, and I didn't know myself. But I ran off with a knowing air and, like a parrot, again repeated my clever word. I loved repeating words which caught my fancy.

We used another funny nickname in our yard: 'wood louse'. This is an insect which is found only in damp places, such as cellars. This nickname belonged to another boy named Slavka, who was also my age. He lived in the same building, but in a deep cellar, four metres deep. There was one terrible episode connected with this 'wood louse'; I can remember it in all its details. There were more than just wood lice to be found in the cellar: there were big rats, too. I was walking along not far from the cellar and suddenly I could hear a terrible cry coming from it. I went over to it and saw Slavka the wood louse quite beside himself, shaking all over with fear. It turned out that the rats had attacked him while he was asleep. His mama was at work and he had no father. He was all alone with the aggressive rats. As he struggled desperately against them, a crowd gathered, hearing his cries. Bitten all over, one ear gnawed round, he was begging for help, and weeping and yelling. At last someone brought a ladder, lowered it and brought him upstairs. The door to his room had been locked.

I remember that this Slavka always chased me with a dead rat, holding it by the tail and flinging it at me, which frightened me terribly. I would begin to shake the moment I caught sight of him and his dead rat. How could he even hold them!? I was horribly afraid even of mice. For some reason there were dead ones lying on the window sill of our flat every day; in all likelihood the boys tossed them up there. Once we found a purse on the window sill. Someone had answered the call of nature in it, clambering up the wall by various projections to the second floor especially for this purpose, and then he had waited until we got up. It happened to be Sunday. Father went over to the open window and saw the purse, which pleasantly surprised him. He opened it impatiently, and then gasped and cursed: he had stuck his hands into liquid muck. A chorus of wild boys roared with laughter: this was a triumph for them. My father was generally at war with the boys in the yard. They used to shout beneath our windows and break the glass, and I remember once he chased them with an axe, wearing nothing but his drawers; but he didn't catch anyone.

One morning I saw a white mouse on the window sill. It caught my fancy and I felt no fear of it, but it turned out to be dead. Otherwise I would have looked after it and put it into a box to bring it up. Being small, I thought that as I didn't have any dolls at the time, this little mouse would take the place of a doll. As I had no dolls, I used to play in the sand. I built pyramids, tunnels and garages out of it, and even modelled little people and made pies and various other dishes for them. Or we might play the following game: we would collect beautiful bits of glass, and, when the others weren't looking, another girl and I would hide them in different parts of the yard, burying them in shallow holes. Later, sometimes we would accidentally find ourselves again near these forgotten holes, which were covered over with earth, and we would make a special search for what we had buried; and little by little we would unearth our secret treasure, as we called it. We were in ecstasy as we did it, just like archaeologists discovering a lost civilization.

One day a new boy – handsome, with thick black curls – turned up amongst the boys. His name was Zheńka. He fitted into the life of the yard fairly quickly and even became the boys' ringleader. He was also a bully. He soon acquired a nickname: they called him the 'coachman'. I don't know why; he was simply the 'coachman'. This didn't offend him, though on the whole he spared no one. He soon learned who had what nicknames, and he used them right and left. Of all the nicknames, mine was especially to his taste. He really licked his lips when he called to me: he liked my nicknames 'sprat' and 'Tatar' that much. He used to make terrible faces, and wriggle and spit, but I remember thinking that, in spite of his mockeries, if he had not been such a bully I could have fallen in love with him. But we didn't use the words 'fall in love' in the yard; we said 'get tangled-up'. Zheńka the coachman was not with us long, disappearing just as suddenly as he had appeared.

One day there was a terrible uproar in the yard. I was on the third-floor landing and saw everything. A strange-looking woman with dishevelled hair was yelling hysterically at someone and clutching Zheńka incessantly. He could not have known what was happening. He looked surprised and blank, as if he didn't even know this strange woman who was clutching him with her tenacious hands. Slobber was dripping from her mouth, and there was foam on her lips. She looked rather like a gypsy, being tall with black, curly hair, though her face was very white. I knew that his mother was a different person entirely: her name was Raya, and she wore her hair combed forward and had doll-like painted eyelashes. He also had a grandmother who was a rubbish-picker. She used to collect rags and bits of paper from the rubbish-heap and sell them for re-use. Day and night she rummaged through the rubbish-heap. Once I didn't notice her bending over the rubbish-heap and emptied refuse on her. Oh, the cries and insults – 'Tatar' etc., etc. – as she brandished a stinking rag under my nose. She always smelled rotten; I don't know how her painted daughter and Zheńka put up with her.

I have digressed a bit; I was talking about the strange woman.

She went on swearing at Raya for a very long time. So, Zheńka was the apple of discord between two women who had laid claim to him. But he himself just looked blank, understanding nothing, as before. The woman was terrifying in her wrath. A large crowd had already gathered to listen to the scene.

Someone said, 'What do you want to bring up a child for, you crazy woman? You'll kill your child, or drive him mad.'

She took the apathetic Zheńka into her arms again – he was such a big boy – and kissed him madly, asking him, 'You do love me, don't you? You'll come with me, won't you?' Then she began to howl, melting into bitter tears. Next, she tore herself away from him and began to swear obscenely at Raya. I still have absolutely no idea which of them was the real mother and which the alleged one. Since this same woman took him away – he still understood nothing that was going on around him – she must have been the mother after all. So, Zheńka disappeared. He might have turned into a fine lad, or so it seemed to me at the time.

Camps of gypsies very often turned up. Everyone was very afraid of them: they said that they stole children. I always thought it strange that they should steal children when they had heaps of them themselves. Later, there were rumours that gypsies drank the blood of small children, because it was said to be very delicious. But, as I recall, they turned up so often simply to tell fortunes, using various tricks they had. They also swindled small amounts of money out of naive people; and if anything lay in temptation's way, it was sure to be stolen by the gypsy children.

I used to be very afraid of gypsies: I was frightened by all the terrible stories about them. My friend Nadya always talked to me about them, probably repeating what she had heard from her parents. She was my only playmate who treated me at all well, this Nadya, with her dark blue eyes and big, cow-like eyelashes, which were absolutely straight, like sticks. After her, other playmates began to turn up. Of course, I always came in last in games, and I had no prestige whatsoever, but they let me play games with them all the same. We had various games. A lot of us, twenty or so, would get together and play these games, hide-and-seek, for example. We would hide in different yards, and each game lasted a long time, because you were always afraid that you would be the last to be discovered: whoever was last became the leader and had to look for everyone the next time, wherever they might have hidden themselves. A whole hour might pass before you found everyone. Sometimes things ended in tears or exhaustion; sometimes I got bored and secretly made off home. Then they would make me search again the following day. It was a tiring game, though interesting. They used to hide in other yards, in clever nooks, and in garrets and deep cellars where the sun never penetrated and there was no electric light during the day; there were mere flickers of daylight at the beginning of the corridor, near the entrance. How could the tenants live there? They turned into cellar rats.

The starry sky

I loved playing with a girl from the house next door; her name was Tanya. I can't remember how we first met – perhaps it was during game time. I liked her: she was a very beautiful girl, with blue eyes and beautiful arc-like brows, thick chestnut-coloured hair, pink cheeks and juicy lips. She treated me as an equal, and won me over as a result. I liked visiting her: her parents were always at work and we could do as we liked. She had a little brother, whom she bossed despotically. She was always pinching him, but he was really nasty, always pestering her and telling tales. He had enormous ears, like a donkey. Tanya used to pull him by the ears because of all his pranks and tale-telling. We would send him outside and play by ourselves.

We were very fond of playing hospital. We had various so-called medical instruments: a small glass shovel, a measuring glass and a pipette for nose drops. We used a school pen to give ourselves 'injections', scratching the skin in various places and afterwards bandaging ourselves. We also played maternity hospital. One day I told her enigmatically, 'Do you know, Tanya: I've found out where babies come from. Mama told me that if you take a man's arm, there will be babies. But I didn't believe her. Then one of my aunts told me that you can buy babies at the market. When you grow up you can choose for yourself: any one you want. I believed her and said that I would be sure to buy myself a beautiful little girl, and I would sew lots of pretty dresses for her.' At this point I shut my eyes pensively. 'But what do you think, Tanya? Where do babies come from?'

She laughed and said, in an authoritative tone, with the look of someone older, 'Ha! I know better than you do where children come from. Papa and mama sleep together, they kiss and embrace, and later mama's belly swells, and papa takes her to the maternity hospital, and there they rip her belly open and take out the baby. Let us play maternity hospital, too. I'll operate first, and you'll be the patient; then you can be the doctor, and I'll be the patient.'

She told me to strip, and I lay down. For some reason it was cold, like in a hospital. She pricked my forehead with her pen and asked if it hurt. Then she daubed it with valerian drops – we had no iodine. She had got long tweezers from somewhere and gently examined my belly, externally of course, and then proceeded to basics: the extraction of the infant. She had a doll ready and pretended to pull it out of my belly. Then she quickly wrapped it up and began to waul, the way babies do. Here I turned into an infant, and she into a mama. I, too, began to waul, imitating Tanya. We began to play mother-and-daughter: she fed me from what was supposed to be a baby's bottle, the pipette taking its place. She put me to bed and pretended to go off into the kitchen to cook. Then we pretended that papa had come home and mama was chatting with him, telling him that I had a poor appetite. It was all very realistic. We liked playing like this. Then we exchanged roles and began all over again with 'hospital'.

Afterwards we used to spy on Tanya's old, painted neighbour as she waited for her man to arrive. (She looked like an old, well-preserved actress, and was of short height and lived alone.) She had rouged herself painstakingly beforehand – in the narrow passage beside the kitchen there stood a large basket full of empty face-cream jars. At last the bell rang, the scented neighbour went to answer it, and in came Tanya's brother; whereupon with a ferocious look on her face she went off to her own room. She never talked to anyone in the flat and always walked with her head tilted back proudly, pursing her haughty painted lips. When her sweetheart finally arrived, she would begin regaling him with various titbits and wines, and we used to tiptoe barefoot up to her door and take turns pressing ourselves to the keyhole. Sometimes we laughed right through the keyhole. Then we would disappear, also on tiptoe, into Tanya's room.

On winter evenings I loved to go sledding. Sometimes I

would sled downhill all by myself; other times we would all go downhill together, or my neighbour Nadya and I would take turns giving each other a push. I always liked to lie on my back on the sled, looking at the sky. Sometimes the sky would be completely covered in stars of different magnitudes. While I lay there it seemed to me that the sky was infinitely deep, and that I was floating across the sky and could reach any star. I felt dizzy with pleasure and would fall off my sled into the snow. I would beg Nadya to push me again, but an agreement is an agreement, and it was my turn to push her. Once when I was lying on the sled and Nadya was giving me a push, the starry sky was suddenly obliterated by the dark and ominous high-booted figure of Zheńka ('Shag'), a fellow from our yard. Seeing that I was lying on the sled, he kicked me in the nose with his boot and knocked me off, railing at me into the bargain, calling me a Tatar and forbidding Nadya to push me. 'And if I catch you doing it,' he added, 'I'll kick your face in, too.' Then he calmly withdrew, striking the cobbles with his boots. Blood was pouring from my nose and I could see stars, but I still couldn't cry. I fell into momentary unconsciousness, but then when Nadya bent over and asked whether I was hurt, I broke down and cried from acute shame and pain. I clenched my fists, but even while doing this I felt my impotence in the face of this lanky fellow – and, what's more, a Russian. Even if I had told his mother, nothing would have happened to him. I went home, and when mama saw me she became alarmed. I told her what had happened and she went off to see his mother, but his mother just listened calmly and apparently did not even punish him, because he went on beating me, spitting in my face and calling me a Tatar. But I also called him names, like 'shag'. I thought this an offensive nickname. Then I called him a Russian, and he became even more incensed. He was some four years older than I, very big, but stupid. Later on, he landed up in a mental hospital.

I had many persecutors. One such enemy was my neighbour Vovka, nicknamed 'the beast'. Their door was next to ours. He always spat at me whenever he saw me, and there was always that irksome name 'Tatar'. He had a very mean mug and always behaved very aggressively towards me, but with the other fellows he restrained himself, keeping his tail between his legs. He was a coward. One day he sat down beside me wearing a sly look on his face. He started to push me off the bench, but then he got bored messing about like that and began imperceptibly to chop off my dress with his hatchet. When I got up, half of it was already gone. I cried bitterly and went home. I did not have another one. I arrived home in dangling tatters.

There was one girl in our yard nicknamed 'chichira'. How she came to have such a nickname, I don't know. She was older than I by some five years. She was very nasty and vicious, and was always fighting with everyone. She was very ugly besides. We disliked each other. She always enjoyed taunting me. It was she who had long before given me bread and slaked lime from the rubbish heap. One day by chance we found ourselves together in the communal lavatory which was situated on the first floor. The lavatory had a cement floor. Along the wall there were stone platforms projecting from the floor, with several holes in them – four, I think. They were all filled with muck which overflowed the rim. They were always obstructed. Sometimes even the corridor was flooded with muck, and the plumber came very rarely, if at all. There was an obstruction again that day, because no one had flushed after himself. The walls were filthy, and everywhere one could see the fingermarks of people who did not use paper but wiped themselves with their hand, and then wiped their hand on the wall.

So, it was my bad luck to come across this 'chichira'. She was there when I came in, but it was too late for me to retreat, having crossed the threshold. I sat down right beside her, where it wasn't flooded. She couldn't bear my being so close and began to tease me by calling me 'Tatar'. Petrified with fear, I replied in turn, 'Chi-chi-ra. . . .' She couldn't bear it any longer and pushed me into the hole, which was almost overflowing. I fell in practically up to my ears, though my legs were sticking out. Using my hands, I slowly managed to crawl out. My dress was dripping, and every sort of filth was pouring off. I shall never forget it. I can't remember if she was punished afterwards – probably not. I arrived home in a pitiful state. Mama was out; and, shaking with resentment, I took everything off and howled and howled. It was always the older ones who tormented me. Boys and girls my own age I might perhaps have repaid in their own coin, but as it was I was conscious only of my own impotence.

School

School tomorrow! Everything is ready for school, except my white apron. The day before yesterday someone's mama gave me a white pinafore: my own mama couldn't afford to buy one, and I didn't have any flowers to give to the teacher. The night before I kept thinking about school – about how I would meet other girls and what they would be like, and what my teacher would be like, and how she would treat me, and I thought: tomorrow can't come quickly enough. I didn't want to fall asleep – I was too excited about tomorrow morning. I also thought that since my mama was going to have a baby, it would be interesting to know whether it would be a girl or a boy.

The morning arrived. I was woken up by mama's moaning, and she suddenly said that I wouldn't be going to school that day, but instead would be going with her to hospital. I collapsed: so much excitement and so many happy expectations, and now a surprise like that! I couldn't even find words for a reply. I put on my old dress, and we went off. She also took along a young girl named Lida who was flat-faced and fat. She had been a nurse since the age of fifteen. She had no parents and her brother had turned to theft and was doing time. So she kept herself alive by whatever work she could find, being looked after by the various people for whom she worked as a nurse. There we were, the three of us, walking along on such a beautiful morning. The sun was shining and it was still warm, although there were yellow leaves whirling overhead, while the thin morning mist had begun to disperse. We began to encounter girls in white aprons with flowers in their hands, and boys in their new suits, tightly belted in.

Mama wanted to go to the Grauerman Hospital which was not far from us, being fairly near the former Dog Ground. The houses there have now all been demolished, leaving only the hospital. Mama began to feel worse and worse and she kept on stopping. There wasn't much farther to go, but when we got some fifty metres from the hospital she couldn't bear it any longer. Lida carried her into a doorway, and, hidden in the corner, mama began to give birth. She told Lida to keep me away. She managed in time to spread out her plush jacket under herself. It was soft. I ran off excitedly with Lida to get help. We called to someone in the house, but she was very frightened by this and ran off in confusion to a neighbour. At last we thought of telephoning for an ambulance, although we were only fifty metres from the hospital. Finally an ambulance arrived from a distant part of town. We drove all the way across Moscow, shaking up my sick, moaning mama. A young doctor held the baby and mama was even able to see that it was a girl. She was named Khalida, but in Russian she was called Galya.

So that was what was meant to be my first day of school and I was rather vexed that I hadn't experienced it. When I arrived at school on the second day, everyone in class already more or less knew each other, while there I was, feeling alien, unexpected and totally unnecessary. I also arrived after the bell, when they were all already seated at their desks. Although I was in the register, the teacher sternly asked me my name, repeating her question several times. I had probably answered very softly, for I was a bit frightened by the large size of our class, which looked at me with eighty pairs of eyes. As it turned out, I wasn't the last pupil, for several girls arrived after me; maybe they had been ill, maybe they were simply new arrivals. The teacher turned out to be young, as I had thought. She had a dry face, hard to the point of asceticism. It would be difficult for me to say whether she was beautiful. Such dry, typically teacher-like faces wouldn't appeal to me now, though she had a good figure in her beautiful dark-blue dress, which was close-fitting at the waist and lightly flared below. She did her hair with the utmost care: part of it she combed forward almost on to her forehead, while the rest hung down to her shoulders in a luxuriant pony-tail. A lot of women used to wear their hair like that: it was the style.

It would be fair to say that I did not like my teacher. On the whole I was afraid of teachers. Just as, when I was still very small, I had been afraid of the ceiling-high woman in the dark cellar, so I was afraid of teachers, like bugbears, and I could see nothing human in them. So, after the very first lesson, I already wanted to go home. I always anticipated the bell with pleasure. During the break I might have been able to have a rest from the authority of the teacher's stony face, but you couldn't rest during the break either, because they made everyone walk round the gymnasium in pairs; and during this time my teacher talked with the other teachers and kept on glancing at us sternly as we walked. We were supposed to walk quietly, and at a measured pace, but at least we were allowed to talk to each other, though not loudly. If any pair misbehaved, they were separated, the pairs were changed, and the new pairs walked around the circle together pouting. Some remained in the classroom with lunches brought from home – sandwiches and apples, for example – and slowly ate them at their desks. But I had no lunch. I went to school almost famished and watched my neighbours enviously as they ate their lunches. Sometimes those who didn't want to finish their lunch would share them with me on the teacher's prompting. I never had a lunch to bring, but some of the girls from rich families would prick their apples with a pen – the sharp end – and extract apple pegs from the holes, and then re-insert them with the other end of the pen, thereby turning their apples into spiny hedgehogs. I would have liked to eat one of them. I looked on and very nearly cried.

I didn't listen to the teacher very well during lessons. Often I didn't hear her at all, and consequently I would not do what I was supposed to do and wrote the wrong things. I lapsed into a kind of reverie, my thoughts being as follows: now wouldn't it be nice if papa made soup today and mama got out of hospital soon? Papa said that I am to go to hospital alone today and take some sweets, and I shall have a bite to eat at the same time, for of course papa will give me something. I want to see my sister; papa said that she is very pretty. Now I have two sisters and a brother. I am a big girl now and can help mama to bath my little sister: she will be my live doll. But suddenly the teacher comes up to me from behind and pushes my head down on to the desk, and in a cruel voice in which there is nothing human, repeats over and over again, shaking my miserable head, 'What am I going to do with you? What are you thinking about? Why aren't you writing? Look at the blackboard and write! Do you want to be punished? I'll throw you out if I ever see you yawning at your desk again!' I don't like you, I thought. I want to go home. I don't want to go to school.

In the third term, my teacher, having decided once and for all that I was incapable of grasping anything, resolved to get rid of me. After all, she still had more than forty other little girls in the class, and there was no time to explain things individually and to look after each one. So she decided to send me to a special school for mentally retarded children. She gave me a large envelope containing a letter to the director of this school, and I set off, little suspecting that I was carrying my own sentence in the envelope, for to go to a special school was considered a great disgrace. When I arrived, the director chatted with me, questioning me very intently, and then said that this was no place for me, and that I should go back to the school where I had been and continue there, as only subnormal children went to this school. 'Here, have a look' – and he showed me a boy with a strange, idiotic face and tiny little eyes; I think now that the boy must have been suffering from Down's syndrome. So I went back to my school, to my teacher's displeasure.

She always put me on public display when my face and hands were completely covered in ink; even before I had written anything at all, I somehow contrived to spatter not only my face and hands, but my hair as well. I looked very untidy: my hair was uncombed and, although short, always dishevelled, my socks were always down, my boots untied, my ears dirty. I always let our section down: the girl chosen to be 'nurse' would walk along our row every morning and examine everyone's hands and ears, and she would always complain to the teacher about me, and the teacher would look at me threateningly. 'It's you again,' she would say, 'always you'; and then she would add that tomorrow I had better turn up clean, or else she would send me home. We also had a prefect in our row – one was chosen in each row from amongst the best pupils – and every day before lessons began she would look at the exercise books in our row and report who had done her work poorly, and who had not done it at all; more often than not I was one of the latter.

I remember that I loved handwriting. I learned very quickly how to trace out each letter – very beautifully, in fact. I used to feast my eyes on my own letters, writing so painstakingly that I unwittingly stuck out my tongue while doing it. The teacher always praised me and showed everyone how well I wrote. I had such a good hand that I even felt I wrote better than the teacher. I was so keen that I began to try to write like an adult, and that was the only reason she ever gave me a lower mark, because adults write any old way, taking no account of the rules of calligraphy. The teacher began to make frequent corrections in my work, because my letters sometimes went slightly above the line indicated and sometimes below. But later on I went back to writing as before, tracing my letters painstakingly, turning them into words and sentences; I found that interesting. On the whole, I loved writing passionately. In my third year I loved writing out dictations. I liked picking out the words and arranging them on paper. I tried to write faster than anybody else. I would write out a sentence and put my pen down noisily, waiting for everyone else to finish writing so that the teacher could dictate a new sentence. I made practically no mistakes – I must have a good visual memory – and remembered how every word was spelt. Dictation was my passion: I often received 'fours' and 'fives' in it. It is very interesting that the artist Anatoli Zverev writes that he passionately loved taking down dictations and he also loved handwriting.

But for some reason I hated arithmetic, and I received 'twos' and 'threes', and sometimes even 'ones'. It was difficult for me to understand the meaning of a problem; sometimes when I got bored trying to guess what one meant, I would look at the figures and, without thinking, attempt to do something with them. The teacher would clutch at her head as she watched me trying to deal with the figures, and then in a fury she would write enormous 'ones' across everything.

On the whole, it was difficult for me to get used to anything Russian without some kind of preparation. I had decided to break once and for all with the Tatar language: first, it hampered my studies; second, I simply did not like my own Tatar language. It seemed ugly and common to me, maybe because I did not know literary Tatar. I began to speak only Russian at home, with absurd results: my parents spoke to me in Tatar, and I answered them in Russian. I was the eldest child and set an example – albeit a bad one, perhaps – to the younger children. So my little brother and sisters, following my example, likewise answered our parents in Russian; on the whole, they assimilated faster than I did in this respect. Although I renounced Tatar, I continued to hate the Russians for being hostile and pernicious. Mama described them well when she said they have no face; this sounds much more picturesque in Tatar. And it is true: they have no face, nor – so it seemed to me – is there anything human in their faces, no smile, no cosiness perhaps. Their faces were all insipid – I soon discerned this – in contrast to Muslims, perhaps because they have lost God, and their faces no longer bear His radiance. Mama and papa always taught me to keep away from them – 'godless ones', they called them. In this respect I always felt a sense of estrangement from Russians, as well as a feeling of self-respect. Because of their hatred I shrank into myself more and more and kept aloof from children my own age. It was painfully difficult for me to get used to them. I had no friends at school, though I did have some at home, but it was as if they were doing me a favour by playing with me. One could sense a boundary: they were Russian, and I was a Tatar – like Americans and blacks.

One day my teacher suddenly announced that several pupils on a long list would be fed free in the canteen, and she distributed coupons for free lunch. I, too, received a coupon. There were, as I recall, about five of us out of the entire class, and during midday recess we were led down some narrow, dimly lit stairs. We entered an equally dimly lit room, and there on a table stood several glasses of milk. We approached with our ration coupons, which bore the principal's signature, and showed them to the canteen lady, Auntie Nyura, who assigned us our places. They served Russian salad on small plates. While they were counting the number of glasses of milk and plates of salad against the lists, one hungry and excited pupil in her impatience accidentally knocked over two whole glasses of milk with her oversleeves. She had extremely voluminous oversleeves. Very likely her mama had been generous with the material to be sure that the uniform would not tear. There were quite a few of us hungry girls gathered together from the various forms; we all looked truly pitiful, with our thin, yellow, and at the same time transparently bluish faces. We were really so famished that we didn't notice how quickly we devoured everything. I could have eaten several more portions myself. The next day we went there quite boldly; in fact, we ran, leaving the teacher behind, shoving one another as we rushed towards the canteen, falling over and stumbling against the high threshold. I in particular used to fall; the quicker girls often knocked me down, although I, too, hurried, in order to have time to finish eating before the bell. They fed us for roughly a year and then for some reason they stopped. Maybe it turned out to be too expensive for the state. I don't know. But I was very sorry they stopped.

Amongst us small children class differences had already begun to make themselves felt. The well-off girls were friends only with other well-off girls, and they looked upon the poor girls with contempt. The teachers, too, paid more attention to children from better-off families and were friendlier to them.

One day the parents' committee met to discuss the need to help children in straitened circumstances. Anyone who had unneeded clothing or footwear was to give it to the needy children. 'Take her, for example' – and the teacher mentioned my name – 'she has absolutely no shoes to wear to school.' It was true: I had nothing. My boots had fallen to pieces, and my toes were sticking out of them. Later, on my way to school, the soles fell off completely, leaving only the uppers. I took off my boots and went to school barefoot. I remember that everyone at school was amazed. I told the teacher everything and she asked whether anyone had spare boots – not new ones necessarily, but not torn, either. I could hear someone's fawning voice: she might be able to bring some boots, but she would have to ask her mama first. This girl was an honours student and she always thrust herself forward, sucking up to the teacher; there was something unpleasant about it. At last she brought me the boots, but I felt very uncomfortable about having to put on somebody else's boots in front of the whole class, with everyone looking at me. Once somebody brought a fur coat to class for me. It was ginger with stripes. True, it wasn't new and was even somewhat threadbare, but I was really pleased with it. I was very happy, for ordinarily I could not even have dreamed of having such a coat. I had no warm clothes at all. Had it not been for the coat, I would have had to go through the whole winter without a winter coat. Even so, I continually suffered from tonsillitis.

We had a singing teacher in our school. He was fairly old and looked like a scientist or philosopher, with his long hair and large, observant eyes. He always wore a dark grey suit, and during lessons he amused us terribly, making faces at us whenever he criticized or teased some poor pupil. Everyone would laugh. When he spoke he stammered slightly, but he sang with great zeal, and rather well; he was a good teacher, though for some reason no one listened to him. We regarded singing rather scornfully, and everyone considered singing class as a kind of amusement when we could laugh or make a row. For some reason I was the only one to take my teacher seriously, running through my scales diligently, always the first to answer any question on music. I greatly enjoyed singing, although the songs were always the same and not very interesting. I remember we always sang a song about Stalin, then we would sing 'Stalin and Mao hear us' – I think the name of the song was 'Moscow-Peking'; we also sang 'We are for peace', 'Singing helps us to live and build' and 'Native land, beloved for ever'.

We were taken to music class in formation. The auditorium in which the lesson was held was two storeys high. As we approached the auditorium door, we could already hear the teacher playing some patriotic march. He always played a march, and we always had to march to our places. When the boys began attending classes with us things became much livelier. They were clever at various tricks and pranks. I recall that whenever we sang patriotic songs the boys always garbled the words. For example, instead of 'Thank you, comrade Stalin', some of the boys would sing, 'Take a piss, comrade Stalin'. They played lots of pranks like this. No one sang in tune. Some would sing, while others farted or mooed; some even kept totally silent, while our nice, funny teacher went on directing our discordant chorus. Our music lessons were generally pure anarchy: everyone did as he wanted. Of course, sometimes our teacher would be relatively successful in getting the chorus going, when suddenly everything would fall silent, the piano would go still, and the teacher – and, with him, everyone who had been singing – would look at those few pupils who, taking advantage of the serious singing, had started launching paper aeroplanes. The teacher, whether in anger or merely pretending to be angry, would begin by staring at them, admiring the way they went on launching them, oblivious of his glare; then one of them, noticing him, would signal with his eyes, and the others would blush to the roots of their hair. The teacher would articulate, syllable by syllable, 'Get out immediately!' Of course, he must have been beside himself from such a lack of attention.

I have happy memories of those singing lessons. It is a pity that later on our headmistress dismissed him for his cheerful disposition and drunkenness; for sometimes he did arrive drunk for lessons. But he was one of our best teachers, if somewhat eccentric. When you met him by chance in the corridor, he would always be humming music, and he would look at you strangely, as though he wanted to frighten you. This was just his manner with pupils.

Then a new teacher arrived. She was always teaching us lyrical songs, like 'In the forest a little fir tree was born, in the forest it grew . . .', and we also sang about snowy roads and the Russian winter. She herself was a young woman of a sentimental sort: her mouth was always open and her lips rounded, as if a song were just about to fly out, like a bird. The boys made rows in her presence, too, muddling words and releasing paper aeroplanes – everything they used to do when the previous teacher was there. I listened attentively to what she said, too, and sang assiduously, wondering why the others were not singing; it even made me angry. The boys laughed at my diligence, and everyone teased: 'Ooooh, listen to her sing!' They often used to rub a notebook up and down my spine and shove me to try to interrupt me, but with a trembling voice I would go on singing. Later, I would complain that such-and-such a boy was preventing me from singing, and he would be sent out of the room, but my tale-telling didn't help all that much, and anarchy continued in class.

During other lessons I was extremely inattentive and heard nothing. I was often distracted. I used to draw quietly, behind the other pupils' backs so the teacher wouldn't see me. Soon she noticed this, took away my drawings and put them on her desk; but during the break she said nice things about the drawings, and later I was considered the best graphic artist in the class. They even put me on the editorial board of the class newspaper for the purpose of making caricatures and other drawings. Once I brought to drawing class a rather large drawing of an autumn landscape executed in black pencil – I don't know why black pencil exactly: maybe I had no coloured ones – but the landscape turned out very well. The result was a truly autumnal mood. There were bare trees standing bent over on a knoll; leaves were being scattered by the wind; while in the foreground the earth was all strewn with rocks and the sky was quite dark, brightening only on the horizon. The result was a good picture of an evening sky. This drawing long hung on the classroom wall, and later in our school exhibition in the assembly hall. After that everyone began to think of me as a talented artist. More than anything else I liked drawing people, beautiful women. The girls even commissioned me to do pictures of beautiful women, and afterwards they would cut these women out and think up various costumes for them, and then cut out the various whimsical costumes and long-trained gowns which they had drawn and dress the women up in them. The results were quite interesting.

Drawing, ballet, books, films

My love of drawing began even before I started school and dates from the time when I used to lie ill in bed for days on end, staring at the walls. Suddenly I would notice something resembling invisible designs on them: if you moved your eye a bit, there would be nothing on the walls, but then you would notice a dot, and again you would see the shapes of animals and people. I often saw fantastic, castle-like patterns on the walls. The latter were covered with plain green wallpaper with embossed bands of broken threads, and it was these broken threads that suggested marvellous shapes and entire pictures to me. I would jump up to get a pencil to outline what I saw, but when I got back into bed I had already lost what, with such joy and wonder, I had previously found. Then I found it again, but by now there were quite different shapes – sometimes terrible monsters on horseback, sometimes mountains and waterfalls – and I would try as quickly as possible to outline them with my pencil; but when I looked again I could no longer recognize what I thought I had seen. It had all turned into something quite different, as though that fairy-tale enigma which my eyes had penetrated had disappeared, leaving only bare lines in which I could find nothing mysterious at all. I often liked looking at the walls in this way: it was my favourite pastime when I was ill. I continue to see these phantoms: I see some sort of picture in everything I look at, in trees and rocks, for example.

One day I saw a very beautiful label on a matchbox. There was a ballerina on it, and I was really very taken by her. She was standing on one leg – on one toe, it seemed – and the other leg was raised high behind her. She was like a bird and her arms were like wings. This produced such a strong impression in me that I took a sheet of paper and drew the ballerina, then I tried to do what the ballerina was doing, raising my leg and standing on the other leg like a crane. The actual results were different, but all the same I already imagined myself as a ballerina. We often played 'knives' in the yard. This is a game in which two people draw a circle on the ground and divide it in half, and then take turns throwing a knife on to the other person's half, cutting off for oneself a piece of the other person's territory according to the course of the knife. The game goes on until one of the players has no ground left at all. This is a predatory, typically Russian game. As we played, I often drew huge ballerinas on the ground and then checked whether I had drawn them correctly. I would stand facing the sun, and there would be my shadow on the ground. I would strike a pose, imitating the ballerina on the matchbox. Sometimes I would make the other girl do it: I would trace her shadow on the ground with a stick or a knife and then walk along the ballerina's silhouette, following her legs and outspread arms until I reached her head. I liked playing 'ballerina', as I called it. But I can't remember where I first heard the word 'ballerina'.

I wanted very much to become a ballerina, and soon I heard that a short distance from us, in Schmidtovsky Park, there was a House of Pioneers with a large number of different hobby groups, in particular a ballet group. I was not a Pioneer, being only nine years old, but all the same I decided to go there and find out about this for myself. I took my younger sister Sonya and set off for the park. I often went there afterwards to take my sisters for a walk; the park is not far from Krasnaya Presnya. My first impression was very positive. There was an enormous pool for children where swimming competitions were held. On a hill stood a small building, completely green: this was the shooting-gallery. I had no money at the time. To shoot once you had to pay a whole rouble, so it was only rich children who could afford such amusement. Once I found a rouble in the park and went off joyfully to have a shot, and, to my surprise, I hit the rabbit and was allowed a free shot, but my second shot was no good, and I handed back the rifle with acute disappointment.

At last I made up my mind to enter the splendid House of

Pioneers, an old, two-storeyed former manor house surrounded by huge, shady trees. I liked everything about it. I was told that the ballet group was on the second floor and I went upstairs to look for the right door. There was a sign on the door with the name of the group, and inside there was music playing and a female voice counting out in a teacher-like tone, at the same time clapping to the music. Then the music stopped, and a shrill voice yelled something abusively. I stood at the door for a long time listening to what they were doing. I was listening to the music, but it was the same thing repeated over and over again: evidently they were not all doing what they were supposed to be doing. Now, if I were there, I would listen carefully and do things right, I thought. At last the lesson ended, the doors opened, and girls and boys poured out. The girls were dressed in white skirts and tennis shirts, while the boys wore black tights. I went up to the teacher and asked whether I, too, could attend lessons. She said that this group had already been going for some time, a whole year in fact, and I should have come earlier; but then she thought about it a bit and decided to accept me, saying that I would have to have a costume, such as I had no doubt already seen on the girls, and then I could attend class. I was very happy, thanked her and ran off home.

On the way home I felt very upset that I had none of the things that she had told me I would need for class: I had no dainty slippers, and where was I to get a skirt? I was afraid to ask mama. She would no doubt say that she didn't have that kind of money, for even as it was she couldn't feed the lot of us. Of course, I was already prepared for the fact that she would buy me nothing; the skirt would have to be made and mama wouldn't make it. On the whole, everything happened as I thought it would: mama was merely surprised and said, 'What have you thought up now? We've never had any dancers in the family. What can you be thinking of, and where am I to find the money for all this?' I cried and beseeched her again and again, but she would still not agree to make me a costume, although the skirt would not have cost very much; she could have bought a little cheap material, the kind they use for pillow cases, and made it in an hour. It wasn't so expensive, and she could have done it if she had been able to understand me, and

I might have been a ballerina now. I still regret not being a ballerina, but it is too late now: even though I am supple, I still can't do things that small children do easily. True, at nineteen I joined the ballet group of the International Theatre of Moscow University. I had not been at it very long, only about six months, when unfortunately I sprained my foot so badly that I had to go into hospital and discontinue my lessons. I remember that during lessons some of the others could not believe that I hadn't studied before. I found this very flattering. I was really very confident during lessons, as if I had studied nothing but ballet the whole of my life. I used to arrive before anyone else and was prepared to go on practising until I was utterly exhausted. My tiredness merely inspired me further. I regretted only that I had lessons just twice a week, for an hour each time.

I read few books as a child. I drew more than I read. I liked even more to give myself up to daydreams, and I always preferred fairy tales: I particularly liked *Cinderella*. For some reason I felt very close to this fairy tale; and in my dreams I wanted to meet a prince with fair hair and blue eyes, and he would take me far away. I always wanted to be beautiful and I wanted my prince to love me for this. As for the prince, I felt that he would have to be not only handsome, but unusually intelligent; and later this prince was suddenly transformed in my mind into a ballet dancer, and I would dance with him, but our audience would not yet know that we loved each other. I also liked *Robinson Crusoe*, *Gulliver's Travels* and *The Adventures of Huckleberry Finn*. I loved reading Aleksandr Grin: his fantastic world was particularly to my taste. I also remember much later reading A. Dumas's novel, *The Count of Monte Cristo*. I would enjoy reading this novel again even today.

The books which I read came from the library. It was not far from school, in an old house on Vesnin Street. One day I joined it. What I did not like about this library was that when children exchanged their books, the librarian always asked what the book was about, and what they thought about it. But I didn't like talking about my impressions. Books were often foisted on me in which the heroes always stood out very strongly, imposing themselves as it were on the reader and this made them repellent to me. Of course, I couldn't say anything to the librarian. My tongue did not seem to me to fit my mouth very well; it didn't hang properly. I couldn't speak very well and was very ashamed of this; when I did begin to speak, it was difficult to understand me and difficult to hear what I was saying, so softly did I speak, as if afraid of my own words. I blushed to the point of tears because I couldn't speak properly, and everything sounded so tongue-tied that I would suddenly fall silent and stand hanging my head.

I did not like books which were foisted on me, like Babayevsky's *Cavalier of the Gold Star*, Fadeyev's *Young Guard*, Gaidar's *R.C.W.* (Revolutionary Council of War) and many other books with pseudo-heroic heroes. They have left no mark whatsoever on my memory. They all seemed too ungenuine, too pretentious, with their obtrusively positive heroes, arousing in me only a feeling of disapproval. As a result, I was automatically filled with sympathy for the negative characters, out of a kind of antagonism to the positive heroes. Thus, I have observed small children to behave as follows: a child may have splendid dolls, lots of stuffed animals and other toys, and yet she may not pay any attention whatsoever to them; but when a little girl presses to her heart an utterly ugly, misshapen doll with a broken leg and dislocated neck, she is following her own quite incomprehensible child's logic in preferring precisely this ugly thing, and treating it with particular love, calling it affectionate names and playing only with it. So it was with me and these books. I did not want what was foisted on me and these heroes seemed repellent to me.

Sometimes, of course, by a happy coincidence I chanced to read a book like *The Prince and the Pauper* or *The Adventures of Tom Sawyer* by Mark Twain. In these books you feel that you yourself are taking part. Everything is simple: on one occasion you may take the side of the negative hero, while on another occasion you may suffer on the side of the positive one. You get excited about all the characters and omit nothing as you are reading. Side by side with these books N. Ostrovsky's *How the Steel was Tempered* has also stuck in my memory for some reason. Pavka Korchagin appealed to me because he was a genuine hero, and the heroine, Tonya, was also genuine. One could easily believe that such a desperate, rather coarse fellow from a simple family could suddenly fall in love with such a well-read young lady from a rich family. If he is capable of falling in love, such as he is, it means that he is already a pretty fine fellow. As a child I believed in such heroes; I felt close to them. That is why I feel that people ought to write more simply and naturally, and there is absolutely no point in over-extolling the positive characters and belittling the negative ones, and inventing for the positive characters super-heroic exploits which I always strongly doubted. I did not want my heroes to stand out sharply in any way; I wanted to decide for myself whom I liked. When I had books with important-sounding titles foisted on me, I automatically began to feel – I had already sadly guessed – that I was being given the same thing again. I began to be a good judge of what was always the same style, and I would ask to be given something different, with a modest, unostentatious title.

I saw few films in my childhood. Other children my age often went to the cinema, but I never had the money: and that is why from time to time I did bad things. For example, without asking my parents I would take money out of their pockets for the cinema, and sometimes I would go to the cinema and, like a gypsy, beg money from passers-by. I would finally accumulate the necessary sum only late in the evening, when there were no more showings that day. But by then I would feel like having some ice cream, so I would buy some and eat it with delight, feeling indescribably happy. Sometimes there would be money from selling apples. Mother and I would go out to sell apples by the piece, and from this mama would give me money for the cinema. Then I felt rich, and besides the cinema ticket I would have enough to buy an ice cream. On these occasions I felt myself quite an independent little girl. The only film which has remained in my memory is Walt Disney's *Snow White and the Seven Dwarfs*, a beautiful and unforgettable film. I would like to see it again. But apart from this I can remember nothing, although I do remember the names of some films which were then very popular: *Tarzan*, which I was unable to see, because I didn't have the money; *The Count of Monte Cristo*, which I didn't see either; and *The Thief of Bagdad*. Everyone in the yard talked about these films incessantly, but I could only listen enviously.

I was very fond of the cinema. I even dreamed of being filmed. One day, as I was strolling along the embankment in the direction of Plyushchikha, I saw a film being shot in one of the side-streets. I don't remember what the film was, but I was amazed by the appearance of the area. It was hard to recognize it: every house bore a bright signboard of a former private shop, factory or firm. For example, I remember a big sign that said: 'So-and-so's (I've forgotten the name) Textiles', followed by 'and Co.'. Cabs carrying rich ladies drove along the clean cobbled roadway, and every stone was distinct. The ragged little boys running after them were dirty and barefoot, their ankle-length shirts were incredibly torn and dangled at their wrists, and their faces were unbelievably soiled. I was surprised and startled by the filming. Then some people appeared in peak-caps, like Lenin's. They had militant looks on their faces and quickly concealed themselves in a doorway where a sign read: 'Kopylev and Co. Print Works'. For some reason I liked that Russia better than the dreary, faceless one of today, with that identical expression on the faces of passers-by. I watched the filming for a long time. I, too, would have liked to have been in the film, if only in the role of someone like myself, who just the day before had been begging passers-by for what seemed to me like big money for the cinema. But no one noticed me.

Relations with my parents

When mama was in hospital, my relations with my father were extremely difficult. We might not talk for days on end, and I got so used to not talking to him that sometimes I forgot that he was there. By the time I was eleven I had ceased to call him 'papa': when I had to ask him something I tried to make do without that traditional and universal word, 'papa'. Evidently he was not pleased by this, although he didn't like me. But I do remember one occasion when I was about sixteen when I called my father 'papa' – maybe the reason was that I was in love with my history teacher – and he jerked his eyes with surprise and even gasped, and then answered me in a kind of strange, warm voice. This had so amazed him that he spoke to me again, and even – or so it seemed – in a rather grovelling voice. But I was so used to managing without this word that to utter 'papa' was an entire revolution for me, not to mention an ordeal. I called him 'papa' shyly and faintly for some time afterwards, until our next conflict, of which there was no end.

I must say that when I was little mama stood up for me, for father was terrible when angry. When he was all set to kill me in his fury, beating me unmercifully with his belt, mama would throw herself upon him with loud cries, trying to shield me; but then father, by now blinded by rage like a bull, would fall upon mama and beat her and then me as well. There was so much screaming in the room it was as if someone was actually being killed. The young ones were all crying and yelling as father towered above us all like a terrible monster, his belt twisting like a snake.

Mama suffered much cruelty from him. She had little love for him and she had not even known him before they were married. It was on such a basis that they began to live their lives together, gradually getting used to each other. Maybe father did love her in his own way. He often joked with her in an amusing manner: for example, he would get down on all fours and chase mama to frighten her. Mama liked that to judge from her happy laughter. She called him a bear because he was very clumsy, but mama quite frequently cried when father was out of the house. Maybe she felt sorry for herself. I don't know. Generally speaking, father was by nature a family man and a non-drinker. He drank only when we had guests and he never left the house to go drinking with anybody. If he had also been intelligent, affectionate and jovial our life would have been quite different. He was very rancorous and malicious himself and not one to forget the malice of others. When mama and papa quarrelled, they had nowhere to go to calm down, and we children all had to listen to this continual abuse and the depressing silence later. Father in particular could remain silent for long periods without giving in. He would lie on his side scowling, and because of this a terrible silence hovered over the room. Then suddenly he would fill this silence with a sharp, invocatory sound, emitted not from his mouth, but from another place. Then mama's lips would part, and she would laugh; and, startled by the strange thunder, we would shout indignantly, 'Mama, it's papa making thunder!' – and we would all attack him at once. Then he would finally soften and begin to mess about with us a bit, and then peace would once again descend on us.

Generally speaking, they would have quarrelled less if they had had more money. I remember that their quarrels often started only because father upbraided mama for spending money, and yet there was nothing to be shown for it, and no money left, and pay day was a long way off, and they would have to borrow money somewhere. But no one was to blame here: mama was never able to allow herself anything extra, only the bare necessities; and if mama finally bought someone boots because their old ones had fallen completely to pieces and they had nothing to walk in, the result was that there would not be enough money left for food for the days remaining till pay day, and one would have to borrow. My parents could never make both ends meet, nor could they ever get out of debt. They both worked, but their wages were insignificant: father earned only 600 roubles working as a stoker for a house-management committee; mama, working at the airport as a dishwasher, earned 300; which comes to 900 roubles for the whole family, i.e. 90 roubles in new money for six persons, which was insufficient for even the most basic food – and what about rent, and clothes?

Mama grew sick of these useless quarrels and decided to do some street-vending after work. Someone advised her to go to the market and buy some fruit and vegetables wholesale and then to resell them in busy places, for instance, near stores. True, this was risky, for the militia would catch such people and take them to the station, but often they simply fined them on the spot. Some militiamen were also mixed up in this: when they caught one of the stall-women, they would fine her without giving her a ticket, simply saying, 'Pay such-and-such an amount!' She would pay in fear, and the militiaman would tell her sternly that he didn't want to catch her again and then calmly pocket the money. He, too, had to make ends meet, his pay was small – perhaps 100 more than my father's – and he probably had a large family. So, to feed us one way or another, my mama used to sell flowers, fruit and vegetables, and in addition, when she left the airport where she had caught a cold, she also worked as a cleaner. She used to get up very early to go to work, then go to the market to make her purchases, then sell them in some crowded place.

When I was still little – perhaps I was in class three or four – I frequently went out selling with mama, and once, when she felt unwell, I took over selling on my own. As ill luck would have it, the weather was very bad that day: it was rainy and cold. I remember distinctly: mama was sick, it was September, the rain was cold and dank, and I had to sell everything. I stood with my miserable green apples, but people passed me by quickly, noticing nothing around them, looking beneath their feet – gloomy people with grey faces, like storm clouds. 'Buy my apples: they're very cheap,' I cried, to attract people's attention, but even so no one looked in my direction: it was as though they didn't hear me. I called more and more faintly, merely shifting my little green apples from hand to hand. I was ashamed of offering such apples, but I was afraid to go home until I had sold every single one. By then I was trembling from the cold, and I wanted very much to eat and get warm. I stood there silently a good deal longer, waiting for someone, perhaps, to buy them from me. How nice it would be if some kind man would turn up and, out of pity, buy all my apples, and then I could go home calmly. I peered eagerly at their faces, trying to guess who exactly would be this good man who was going to buy my apples, but they all passed by without even noticing me. That was the only time I traded on my own. I was almost always mama's guard while she traded. I used to stand a short distance away, looking to see if a militiaman was coming and if one appeared on the horizon, I warned mama quickly and cramming everything into her bag, she would hide in a store or in a women's lavatory nearby. The lavatory attendant even received a modest bribe from the street-traders. Sometimes a militiaman would appear unexpectedly from around a corner and fine somebody or take someone off to the station; while the others, who had managed to make a quicker get-away, recommenced their trading with greater care and caution in another spot.

For all the danger, the takings were very small. I remember that we ate very meagrely on this money: for breakfast we had only tea and bread – when there was butter for the bread, we considered ourselves lucky; for lunch we had soup and then tea; for supper, often boiled or fried potatoes, or some kind of porridge – pearl barley or millet – and again tea. True, father also had soup in the morning, because he did heavy physical work. I remember how mama always counted the lumps of sugar and put them in a bowl. She had fixed the following quota: one lump for everyone, so if you reached out for more you got your knuckles rapped. That is how mama shared out everything amongst us. We children always looked at one another with greed and envy to make sure that nobody got anything extra; and if, as it seemed, someone – I, for example, being the eldest – did get something extra, the younger ones would tear it out of my hands and not let me eat it; I would have to eat it on the sly. It was quite impossible to share a paltry lump of sugar. We always had fierce arguments and quarrels at our table, even coming to blows over a milligram. After we had finished eating, all the food was carefully locked up and as a result we children all hunted after the hidden key. Mama sometimes took a nap and the hidden key would fall out of her pocket. It would be instantly stolen by me or my sister Sonya and would long remain hidden on one or the other of us until, in our parents' absence, someone would open the big bin and take something. We took precisely those things which mama very rarely put on the table – jam, for example – and we would regale ourselves on it, whispering and agreeing that none of us would tell our parents.

Although Sonya also made use of the bin, she still gave me away when the opportunity arose, and then – beware of father! He certainly would not let this pass. He would take his wide belt and start thrashing away until I cried for mercy. But he would say, 'I'm going to thrash you until the blood flows.' As father slowly took off his belt, jangling the buckle, I would stand stock-still with terror, tense all over; and when he held his snake-like belt over me, I would throw myself at him and cling to him like a cat. This only intensified father's anger and he beat me unmercifully with terrible force, literally for the slightest misdemeanour. The main reason, of course, was that I always spied on them, spoiling their nights of bliss. He especially hated me because of this and thrashed me violently. When mama saw this going on, she was afraid that he would kill me, so fierce was his hatred.

After thrashing me he would shut me up in the cold storeroom, where there were rats and mice. I would lie down on some bare boards, utterly exhausted and, weeping bitterly, fall fast asleep; and when I woke up, my body would begin to shake from weeping again and I would even fall into hysterics. I used to bite myself, tearing at the still unclosed bleeding welts. I liked causing myself pain; open-mouthed and wide-eyed, I felt pleasure as I did it. My friend Nadya used to come for me. She would knock on our door and my mama would tell her that I would not be coming out, but I would call to her in tears from the storeroom, begging her to remove the lock, or push aside the bolt, if the door was simply bolted shut. For some reason she would stand in front of the door for a long time, huffing and puffing; she never got the hang of it and opened it only with difficulty. I was grateful to her and glad to see her, my deliverer. We would sit together in the storeroom, and she would ask me what had happened and why I had been beaten and shut up in the storeroom. At first her questions made me cry even worse than before, but then I would show her all my bleeding cuts and big bruises and say over and over again, 'How I hate him, that father of mine!' Nadya would try to calm me down, asking whether I had had anything to eat. I would shake my head and she would run back to her place and bring me some bread which I would eat greedily. Once I had calmed down I would go to her place.

I always wondered why I had been given my parents, and not others. I did not like them at all. I tried, if only for a minute, to imagine other parents – affectionate, rich, cultured ones. While lying in bed at night I would think: after all, there are uncles and aunties who have no children, and I would begin to imagine to myself a cultured uncle with grey hair and a similar auntie, only slightly advanced in years. They had no children and they would take me for several years to bring me up, and then my real parents would feel obliged to take me back. I would be big by then, and would have to go to work to help them: after all, they were short of money. And my uncle and auntie would have made me very cultured. I had already completed ballet school and learned to play the piano, and they were so accustomed to me that they didn't want to give me back to my parents for anything in the world. I had also come to love them very much, so I stayed with them. I could already imagine myself as a young woman. I never had a chance to see anyone of a different culture than that of my parents or our neighbours. I imagined my new parents' house to be old-fashioned and patriarchal, and in such a house one's relations to one another would be tender, without swear words; and the parents would kiss their children tenderly and take walks with them and my parents would understand me.

If I had had such parents, I would long ago have studied ballet and music, but as it was my mama once struck me hard on the head with a glass solely because I had reproached her for not buying me a notebook, for I had nothing in which to do my lessons. After striking me with the glass mama became very frightened. The glass was in the bag with which mama went out to sell sunflower seeds, and it was with this bag that she had struck me. Blood was pouring from my head and simply would not stop. The wash-stand was full of blood and mama did not know what to do. She wailed so much that I became terrified, not because of the blood or the pain, but because of her hysterical cries. At last she decided to wrap my head in a rag and take me to the chemist's, which was not far away. They shaved the hair around the wound, daubed it and bandaged my whole head. I looked like a wounded soldier and still have a memento of it in the form of a bald spot and a bump.

My relations with my parents grew worse and worse. Whenever my father beat me, I would mutter threateningly that I was going to leave them. I so resented my parents that I finally decided to leave home for good in the fantastic hope of finding new parents. I was about nine or ten. It was a Sunday morning in March, the time of year when it is beginning to melt a little in the morning, the sun is delightfully warm, and during the day it gets even warmer; it is only towards evening that everything begins to stiffen with cold, while the dusk is very cold. So I began my search on a sunny morning, taking with me a large chunk of bread and some sugar, and set off, following my nose. Various uncles and aunties passed me by, and I scrutinized them, making my appraisals; and so I walked for a long time, looking at everyone, but no one caught my fancy. I began to feel hungry. I took a hunk of bread from my pocket and ate it. I began to feel frozen. I was wearing nothing but light clothing: an autumn coat, a thin scarf on my head and no mittens; but I did not want to go home. I walked a long way down the embankment, to Presnya, turned right into Schmidtovsky Park, strolled there a while, then went elsewhere, still searching for new parents, but I never found them, and no one noticed me. I turned into a courtyard and warmed myself a bit in a doorway. Then I burst into tears, feeling utterly alone; and for some reason I began to wish that my own mama would find me and clasp me to her breast, but she wouldn't clasp me, although she could be affectionate. Yet in her caresses there was something incomplete – maybe she didn't care for me. Oh, how cold it is!

I wonder if mama will look for me. A door opened in the depths of the doorway, and a beautiful woman appeared. She went out into the courtyard and called to a little girl, most likely her daughter. The woman was undoubtedly cultured. She was wearing a beautiful dress and her face wasn't coarse. I looked enviously at the little girl whom she was leading. The door slammed behind them and I was alone again in the empty doorway. I felt empty and lonely within, too, and all my senses had become deadened, as though I was gradually freezing inside. I sat down, focusing on a single point, and saw before my eyes my terrible father with his snake-like belt and my weeping mama. I suddenly felt very sorry for her. I thought: why, maybe he's beating her at this very moment, or maybe she has been searching for me the whole day, and now she's run off her legs. I shall go home – not because I myself want to go home, but only out of pity for mama. I left the doorway and began to make my way home.

When, after an hour or more, I approached our house, I did not immediately go into the yard but walked for a while along the other side of the street, to let myself be seen. Hardly had I appeared but I was noticed by neighbours who knew that I had been missing since morning. They told mama and she immediately ran to me with frightened eyes, not knowing whether to be glad or not; though somehow she began to speak to me gently. I let her kiss me, trying to behave very proudly and independently so as to show that I could survive without them, and that if I wanted to, I would go away for ever, although I knew that I had no idea where I could go. I returned home with mama unwillingly, into a house I didn't like, to a father I didn't like; but I was unbearably hungry, having eaten almost nothing since morning, apart from that hunk of bread. In spite of hating my home, I still looked forward to a hot supper, a warm room and my bed. I intended to fall asleep slowly, dreaming of the new parents whom I had still not managed to find. Mama took me by the hand, saying over and over again how cold and hungry I must have felt, but I would feel nice at home, I would warm myself and have some hot soup to eat. Indeed, like a watch-dog I was so hungry for something to eat that it did not matter what it was. When I entered the room, father lowered at me and mumbled something like: 'Hmm, so she's turned up: our lost little girl. Why don't you go back where you were?'

And my sister Sonya came up to me and said, not without spite, 'We've eaten without you. There were jam patties. Mama bought them, but she hasn't left any for you.'

Mama began to fuss over me as though I were a new-born baby. She even combed my hair. I'll admit it was pleasant. While she did it she talked affectionately and called me a little fool. Then she removed my soaking wet boots and socks. By and large, all the attention was on me. I only resented her not leaving me any patties. I asked her about it, but she looked at me meaningfully and seated me at the table. First mama gave me some hot soup, then for the next course some fried potatoes, of which I was very fond, and for the third course there were patties and tea. This was a great occasion for me. I thought slyly: mama has probably done all this purposely to earn my love, but I know all her tricks. But, all in all, it was nice to find shelter and warmth of a sort once again. The evening passed very well: I played with the younger children, everything was quiet and peaceful, and my parents talked gaily. I loved gaiety, joy and peace in the house.

My brother Mansur

Five years later, when my brother Mansur was nine and I was fourteen, he decided to run away from home as I had done. He ran away with a friend who had no father. It was the other boy's idea, as I recall. He even had money which he had stolen somewhere. This boy and my brother boarded a train without tickets and got a long way from Moscow, fifty kilometres, but then the ticket collector caught them and turned them over to the militia because they would not even give their names. They would not give their names at the nearby militia station either. There was a children's home not far away, so they were taken there, where they spent several days.

Mama searched for him in panic. She telephoned all the militia stations; then she was informed by headquarters that they were in a children's home. Mama set off with the other boy's mother and brought them back; that was the end of their travels. Mansur did not tell us much about the home, though he did say that for the most part they were hoodlums there, they ate from aluminium basins, and everyone threw spoons at one another. They all went about in formation and worked in joinery shops.

I do not know what happened later to Mansur's friend, but I do recall that his mother even wanted to give him up. He stole money endlessly from her and from other people. His friendship with Mansur came to an end because we moved from Smolenskaya across town to Vernadsky Avenue. Later on my brother also began to play truant and used to disappear for the whole of the day. As he grew up he gradually became aggressive and often attacked father with his fists. He made very poor progress at school, behaved more and more like a hooligan, and beat our sisters, and even me, although I was older than he was. Later, when he was sixteen, he went mad.

Still quite ill after his long stay in hospital, when he returned home he never went out of doors. He had begun to feel shy and afraid of people, and would only sit in his room (we received a three-room flat when I was seventeen), pounding his head and muttering aloud, 'What an idiot I am! What an idiot! I'm an idiot!' By then he drew only very rarely, mainly copying from various textbooks and later putting them forward as his own. Whenever I visited my parents he would show me these drawings with an important look on his face. Still earlier, he decided to write a novel. He wrote one short page which lay in his desk for several years. Later, as a consequence of his serious illness, he began to show signs of megalomania. He called himself a great writer, a great painter, superior even to such an artist as Leonardo da Vinci, to say nothing of me. He always treated my art work very derisively and, assuming an air of importance, always argued that although he was younger than I, he was older in artistic matters. He would ask why there were no lines in my pictures, and why my pictures always contained only barely perceptible, almost dissolving forms. I, too, assumed an air of importance and told him that I was not a draughtsman, making only sharp lines. As a matter of fact, he irritated me terribly when I was still living with my parents. He knew almost nothing, never went to exhibitions, read only science fiction and always argued with great aplomb. To tell the truth, he had something – not talent, but rather an aptitude for drawing.

All in all, I do not think my brother was aggressive by nature, but he had been made so by our parents, who were intolerant of all children's pranks and games. In fact, I recall that as a child my brother was very sympathetic and good, with a strongly marked sense of justice. He was very easily hurt and was consequently explosive in his reactions. I recall how my brother used to bring home various insects and mess about with them for hours, arranging them on cotton wool in different boxes; or else he would bring back lame puppies and kittens which the boys in the yard had been teasing. He wanted to look after them, but my parents used to turn him out along with his animals, saying that insects brought nothing but harm, while dogs ate a lot and there wouldn't be anything left for us. So, his butterflies flew off into the air, while the dogs sometimes barked, sometimes whimpered at my parents' rudeness.

The childhood, adolescence and adventures of my sister Sonya

My sister Sofiya, or Sonya, was two years older than my brother, but she went mad considerably earlier, at roughly eleven years of age. She was much more interesting than my brother. I think that had she not been insane, she would have been quite uninteresting, and would have been like many unartistic people in this dreary, monotonous life. Such people go through life leaving nothing behind them, neither memories nor actions.

Apparently Sonya had been sick from earliest childhood, but no one had particularly noticed it. She was gay and lively, not aggressive like my brother, although for some reason she always attended a special school, the same one to which I had been sent with my teacher's letter. This was a school for mentally retarded children and the syllabus was slower and easier. I recall that when I went there to fetch her, I used to see in the cloakroom degenerates with clenched faces, flat noses and piggy eyes. A lot of the children had these features; and there was my Sonya, a pretty little girl with an intelligent face, and at the time I didn't understand. True, she grasped things fairly slowly, but that happens to everyone sometimes and I wasn't good at my studies either. They praised and admired her at school: she was tall with black hair and big, dark, pensive eyes. She was popular even in the building where we lived, despite the fact that she was a Tatar.

Once, when she was eleven or twelve, mama sent her out into the yard with the rubbish; it was evening. When she returned we were startled by the expression on her face – it was so full of fright – and she was shaking all over and muttering something, but you couldn't make out what.

Mama and I asked her, 'Sonya, what's happened?' She made no reply.

There was indescribable terror in her eyes and she was on the point of bursting into tears, but she told us finally that nothing unusual had happened. We felt strange and I decided to find out what all this meant. I slept in the same bed as Sonya. When we had all gone to bed, I slowly began to question her. At first she said nothing. Then I began to ask some leading questions, implying that perhaps someone had offended or ill-treated her.

After remaining silent for a long time, she suddenly said, 'Don't tell anybody: something bad has happened to me.' Again she said nothing for a long time, but I pestered her persistently, pressing her for her story, and assuring her that I would tell no one. Then, deciding that she could trust me, she began slowly, 'You know, I'm going to have a baby soon. I'm pregnant.'

I was quite taken aback by such a beginning and asked, 'How did you get pregnant? Where? How? Did the wind do it?' I began to laugh, for I didn't believe her.

When I stopped laughing she continued, 'When I went out into the yard to empty the rubbish, Slavka the wood louse was there, running around the dustbins. He saw me and came into the lean-to where the dustbins are and he hugged me in the corner. I broke loose and ran off.'

I asked her in amazement, 'What, is that all? Didn't he do anything more to you than that?'

At this point she went quite silent, and it was impossible to extract anything more from her; and so she fell asleep. I thought that maybe all this was only her sexual imagination: we all experienced it. I think now it was simply that her first menstruation had started early, and that by chance it coincided with the incident by the dustbins and had frightened her by being so unexpected.

The next morning she said nothing to anyone, looked at us all sullenly and was terribly rude to everybody, especially father, although for some reason father always loved her more than the rest of us. I don't know why: maybe she reminded him of my mother in her youth. Afterwards mama often noticed that money was missing and all suspicion fell on Sonya, because this used to happen when the rest of us were out. She began to disappear from the house frequently, returning only late in the evening. Soon afterwards it turned out that she had not gone to school for a long time. Her teacher arrived to try to find out what was the matter. She said that when Sonya had last attended school she had been very strange: she had never been badly behaved before, but now she was a ferocious beast. She complained that Sonya had broken a desk and torn up textbooks. All in all, she was so changed that no one in the class recognized her. The teacher asked us to watch her, because something was happening to her. At night I would be woken up by her conversations: she used to talk in her sleep with someone, swearing in street slang; she would even strike me in her sleep. She used to beat our youngest sister and became so aggressive that mama began to be rather frightened of her.

Once, as we were lying in bed, Sonya suddenly began to talk strangely. At first she was so enigmatic and diffuse that I could not make any sense of it and I kept on asking her to repeat it. I cannot remember precisely what, but she was saying fantastic things: for instance, that she had met a foreign girl whose house was not far from the embankment. She described the house in such fabulous terms, and I simply couldn't say how many rooms there were – you couldn't count them all – and the little girl herself was dressed like a doll, and Sonya had been treated to a lot of different kinds of chocolate. She described certain fantastic, white-coloured apparatus of enormous dimensions. I recall that she was particularly delighted with the telephone on which one could supposedly call other countries, and she said that the little girl had talked on the telephone in her own language. She said that when she was in the flat it was like being in a fairy-tale world, such was her amazement. But later she became confused and it was difficult to connect everything she said, though what she told me produced a fantastic impression.

The following day she suddenly brought back tins with brightly coloured labels, as well as chocolates and white shoes with high stiletto heels. As soon as mama saw these things, she sat down and gasped with surprise, and, as she always did when surprised or delighted, covered her face with her hands like a small child and then clasped them helplessly and asked with fright where it all came from. She took everything away from Sonya at once, thinking that the food was poisoned. At that time all parents forbade their children to accept anything from strangers. Ever since the 'doctors' affair' (1953) rumours were rife amongst the common people of 'doctor-poisoners', Jews of course, and also 'American spies'. But Sonya proved to be much nimbler than mama. She tore the tins and shoes from her hands and ran out of the house with mama running after her. Sonya got all the way to the embankment and was already standing on the bridge, so mama ran on to the bridge, but Sonya, leaning over the railings, threw into the water everything that she had managed to snatch back from mama, just to prevent her from intercepting it. Anyway, mama managed to catch her and bring her home. There she mulled it all over for a long time afterwards, discussing it with father. My parents still think that Sonya went mad from eating this foreign tinned food.

Meanwhile several days passed and Sonya was up to her surprises again, staying out until dark. We were worried that something might happen to her again, but she turned up at last, looking absolutely dreadful, as if she had been through hell: covered in blood, her hair on end, her eyes wild-looking, her face smeared with dirt, her dress torn, and holding a man's bloody sock in her hand. At the sight of her, mama almost went out of her mind, while the younger children woke up and started crying, but Sonya boldly endured our stares and mama's hysterical voice. Then mama calmed down a bit and, saying nothing either to her or to us, began to tidy her up and put her to bed, leaving everything else until the following day; while father showed unexpected tact, saying nothing to Sonya, but barking at us, 'Everyone go to sleep!'

That night I decided to find out from Sonya what had happened to her. She told me that a luxurious automobile had driven up to her and the door opened to reveal a very handsome man inside. 'You know me,' he said. 'I'm the artist your sister has talked about to you. I know your sister very well: she's a talented artist. Get in. I'll take you for a ride.' And Sonya got in. He took her for a long drive out of the city and when they had reached the open countryside he stopped the car and began to court her crudely, and after lengthy resistance he overpowered her in an open field. It was almost night time and there was not a soul around; her cries were drowned in the darkness. Sonya then recounted how he had driven her almost to our district and left her so she had had to walk the rest of the way home. Everything was confused in her account: her attacker was suddenly transformed from an artist whom I knew into a certain Vitya who was very much in love with her and came to see her in the yard all the time; she would go out to meet him, too. Her hatred of her ravisher was suddenly transformed into ardent love. But I know perfectly well that she had invented the artist. She had simply been raped by some ruffian. One day I had told her about an artist, mentioning that he was handsome, and I had also talked about a car, but in her sick imagination everything had got jumbled up; although what had been done to her she related fairly coherently. We never found out who had done it: apparently his name was Vitya, because Vitya appeared in her fantasies more than once afterwards.

Following this incident she finally lost her mind and mama took her to a psychiatrist who pronounced her seriously ill. Mama then showed her to a gynaecologist in order to be absolutely certain – as if it were not already clear – that she had lost her virginity for ever. After this comprehensive examination she was sent to a mental hospital. She spends time there almost every year now, but she lives at home sometimes, too. She was thirteen when all this happened, but she looked like a tall, slender girl of seventeen. All the same, by the time she turned seventeen she had become as stout as a forty-year-old, though she had a young face.

Whenever she came home from hospital, I tried to go places with her. I even took her to the conservatory. She always made me laugh by her absurd escapades, though sometimes I even felt ashamed that she behaved so strangely. She always dragged around a small, but very voluminous handbag from which she was inseparable and when she opened it, out spilled heaps of all kinds of rubbish – breadcrumbs and bits of paper – and sometimes she even contrived to bury a bottle of kefir in it. She would pull a dirty handkerchief out of the bag, and inside it there would always be a small pencil stub, a tiny fragment of a mirror and some scribbled notes; but the chief object in her handbag was a small book, a brochure by some astronomer-academician. She always carried around small books of that sort, for she loved astronomy passionately and even planned to write a large tome about a great discovery of hers of world importance.

So, there she was, opening her bag during the interval, wearing a serious expression on her face and looking at no one as she dragged out the pencil stubs and brochures one by one and put them on the seat beside her. She began searching anxiously for something and everything fell on to the floor. An intelligent-looking man and lady passed by. He noticed an object that had dropped and moved forward a bit to pick it up and hand it to my Sonya. But not on your life! Sonya bent over with incredible haste and quickly picked up the dirty handkerchief. Then she began feverishly rummaging about again, at the same time looking around apprehensively for fear that someone might sit on the seat where her things were lying. She was afraid that someone might snatch such important objects as a small sheet of paper with her latest thoughts and the astronomy brochure. The bell rang for the second part of the concert. Pushing her way excitedly past everyone else, my Sonya ran to a row where she thought there were free places. She rushed headlong, filling everyone around us with indignation. They were all looking at her by then and I felt awkward, but she settled down there anyway and shouted for me to join her, thereby adding to the general indignation, for everyone already had their ears attuned for the music. As soon as the first chords sounded, Sonya, to our neighbours' horror, suddenly began to conduct from her seat, waving her fat arms and mouthing the music. At the next interval she rushed headlong to the platform and began talking to the musicians, claiming that she was a real conductor, and advising them how to play better. Of course I tried to keep as far as possible from her. I did not know what to do – I felt so embarrassed and ashamed; and all the while she kept calling me over. When I reproached her afterwards, Sonya answered coolly, 'What can you expect of a sick person?'

She loved conducting, and not only at concerts, but wherever she happened to be: at home, out visiting friends, or in the street. She liked music and expressed her passion for it with her voice and every movement of her arms. She loved Bach and when she heard his music on gramophone records her eyes would rove madly, then suddenly stop somewhere in unknown space. Her eyes are beautiful and awfully big: there is a black abyss in them. When I got married and went to live with my husband, my sister immediately came to visit us without so much as ringing first. (It was a month when she was not in hospital.) She burst noisily into our room with the whole enormous weight of her monster body, accidentally knocking over my pictures which were standing against the walls. The room was filled with her laughter and a terrible din. She immediately sat down at the piano and began to make music. Playing the piano was her passion, although she did not know a single note and had no idea what each key meant. But she played with great confidence, passionately, to the point of self-oblivion. My husband and I would give her a theme and she would immediately set about improvising. I must say, she had a remarkable gift of improvisation: she used every key and was assured in her playing. At one moment you would hear what sounded like Beethoven's powerful chords filling the courtyard and we thought our piano would burst. Later, she would suddenly switch to something resembling Chopin, and, later still, other powerful notes, now sounding like Bach, would hit the ceiling. While improvising she always said proudly that the music which we were hearing was of her own composition: she was afraid that we would think that it was Bach, Beethoven, or Chopin, and not her own music at all, and that we would give credit to them rather than to her. We were amused by her fears on that score. As I have said, she did not know a single note. Once, to be sure, Sonya pulled out of her bag a dog-eared sheet with notes on it: she said that it was the 'Internationale'. She put it on the music rack and began pounding the keys senselessly, adding that she would soon be entering the Gnesin Institute. She was always making plans of one kind or another.

Besides her musical talent, Sonya had an aptitude for painting, but as she herself used to say, she didn't want to be an artist: this was merely a passion of hers. She often brought us her drawings and water colours. Her drawings were indeed interesting for their strange surrealist composition, particularly her female portraits. I recall a drawing executed on paper of a nude woman reclining, with her head turned towards a top corner and her legs in a bottom corner. Because of her diffidence and naivety, she reminded me very much of the women in Pirosmanishvili's pictures.

Sonya considered astronomy her most important occupation. She read books on astronomy, visited the planetarium, attended lectures there and went to see astronomical films. Although mama gave her no money for the planetarium, this was no problem for Sonya: she would simply steal the money from our parents' pockets when they were not looking. In addition, she not only read popular-scientific pamphlets and attended lectures, but she even made astronomical discoveries, expounding them on the pages of her school notebook. Once she even sent a letter about one of her discoveries to Academician Sedov at the Pulkovo Observatory in Leningrad. Her letter came back with the information that there was no Academician Sedov there. Galya and I read the letter when she was out. It was hard to make any sense of it. One letter of the alphabet was piled on another, and it was such gibberish that I couldn't say what it meant. The first two letters at the beginning of a sentence would be legible, but further on everything ran together and then broke off. I can recall only the following: 'A comet should appear in 1973. It will hit the earth and overturn it.' Strangely enough, this prediction was partly fulfilled, for Kohoutek's comet appeared in 1973, although it didn't overturn the earth.

After getting the envelope back, Sonya pulled out her manuscripts and headed straight for the university, on the Lenin Hills, and waited outside the entrance for a man with a learned air and a big briefcase. When just such a man appeared, she rushed up to him and asked whether he was a scientist. When he answered in the affirmative, evidently realizing with what sort of person he was dealing, she pulled her manuscripts out of her bag with a mysterious air and said that her discovery was set forth there, and that she wanted it to become world-famous and that he should give it to the right person for a scientific appraisal. The scientist listened to her very amiably and then replied that he would be very pleased to help her. He took her manuscripts, put them into his big briefcase, took her by the hand and said that he wanted her to meet his astronomer colleagues, and led her away. They stopped outside a huge grey building. He left her at the entrance, asking her to wait, and a while later he came out accompanied by a woman in a white coat. The very amiable scientist gently led Sonya over to the woman and said his colleagues wanted to talk with her at once about her work, whereupon he hurried off, with an amicable 'good-bye'. The woman led her into her consulting room, questioned her about the manuscripts, asked her address and then spent a long time writing something, after which she telephoned for an ambulance and my Sonya was carried off to a mental hospital. Her manuscripts ended up there, too, thereby enriching her 'case history'.

When we finally located her at the hospital, a doctor told us how she had got there. Sonya was in an extremely depressed state. When we visited her she was unrecognizable: she showed none of her previous vitality and fervour, looked yellow and apathetic, and did not want to talk to mama and me. She could not even recall how she had landed in hospital and was unconcerned about her manuscripts. I do not know what treatment they were giving her, or the others either, but the majority of the patients were as languid as she was. They were very likely being stifled with various medicines whereby the patient forgets everything and is turned into the mere semblance of a person.

The visitors' room was not very large and also served as the patients' dining room and sitting room. There they watched television and during the day occupied themselves with handicrafts: they embroidered, made and dressed wooden dolls, and painted. All their best work was exhibited under glass in this room. That was what they did in the winter time. In summer they were taken out to plant vegetables and flowers. I loved the idea of the patients standing in the middle of the wood, surrounded by meandering paths and flower beds which they themselves had made. There was a large piano in the room and everyone who knew how to play on it, played on it, and those who did not know how played on it, too. This is where my Sonya learned to play with such assurance. During visiting time so many relatives crowded into the room that there were not even enough chairs for them all and there were several standing around each patient. The relatives fed their own sick zealously, even forcibly cramming what they had brought into their mouths, lest it fall into the nurses' and sisters' hands later. The latter, whenever a patient was in a state of shock, used to eat the relatives' presents. There were some patients who did not even hear what their relatives were saying. When they ate, their ears moved like a dog's, and everything that had been brought for several days they would eat all at once. It was terrible to watch them. They were like savages or animals then and their relatives would look on meekly, as though this was the way it had to be now. My Sonya was one of these gluttons, but she was not always like that: it depended on the kind of medicine they were giving her, and as a result her condition was different every time we saw her. The doctors were most likely testing the effect of each medicine on her. After all, this was the Kashchenko Hospital, which was attached to the Institute of Experimental Psychiatry.

The treatment was such, that of a hundred patients, perhaps only one per cent would somehow recover, while the rest were not being cured, but just repaired; that is to say, their illnesses passed from one form to another. In the hospital there are registers stating when the patient arrived, what treatment he underwent, and what medicines he received, and all this has to be kept within a six-month period, whereupon he or she is discharged, although it is obvious even from a distance just how healthy the patient is. For example, when Sonya landed in hospital, she was treated for six months, then discharged, and she arrived home even more ill than before. A few days later she landed back in the same hospital and even the very same section. Once again they started a case history for her and she was recorded as having been readmitted for treatment. It seems that the important thing is not the process of treatment and its general results, but fitting it into this period so as to create the semblance of favourable recovery statistics.

I recall that on one visit Sonya was unusually lively and excited. Her eyes were restless and sparkled feverishly. I almost recognized in her the same person who used to come to our place to play the piano with such vivacity and temperament, the same person who had fussed over her manuscripts. She did not look at mama and me but kept looking at the men who had come to see their wives or children. She took some bananas out of mama's hands and went over to offer them to some men. She went up to the handsomest and offered him one, then said without the slightest ceremony, 'Tell me, please: is it true that I am beautiful? Is it true that I have big hazel eyes and a Roman nose?' She went on offering him the bananas, in spite of his embarrassment. My other sister, seeing what she was doing, dragged her away from him immediately and led her back to us, scolding her along the way; but Sonya merely sniffed scornfully at her. At moments like that she was devilishly beautiful, because, as I see it, this whole illness was a devilish obsession.

I remember one more amusing episode, when one day in hospital Sonya very nearly burned alive her hated ward neighbour. The neighbour woke up to find all her bedclothes in flames. The sister who was on duty in the corridor, hearing her cries and noticing the smell of burning, ran in and saved her in the nick of time; while Sonya, frightened herself, hopped over the beds, jumping on the patients, as she fled the sister. Another sister came to her aid, and they caught Sonya and moved her to the violent section. It is interesting that all the letters that Sonya wrote to us from the hospital began as follows: 'I feel well and hope you are likewise.'

At home after a stay in hospital, she would act passive and languid at first. During her final days in hospital they gave her large doses of sedatives and she would arrive home indifferent, apathetic and uninteresting. She had no appetite and slept round the clock, but when these medicines had worked themselves out of her organism, she would gradually emerge from hibernation and blossom forth. Then she manifested wild fantasies, a talent for painting, or an interest in astronomy, but along with all this there recommenced and even intensified her fierce hatred and suspicion of her parents who did not understand her. She displayed an animal's appetite and ate enough for three persons, thereby arousing our parents' fury. She was unbearable at home. Our place was turned into hell and it would become necessary to put her back into hospital, where they again suppressed her illness with medicines, just as poachers smother fish in a river.

On leaving hospital she would go to an *artel* for work. This *artel* was located in a psychiatric out-patients' clinic, where the patients worked under the supervision of a doctor and a shop foreman. There were sewing machines in the shop and the patients were trained to make bed linen. Later they taught them how to perform more complicated operations, for example, how to make brassières and sanitary belts. This was all then sent to the shops, to the Muscovites' delight, because if this *artel* had not made brassières, who would have made them? Factories do not like having to bother with such trifles: they ruin their specified plan. My Sonya proved to be a very capable seamstress in this *artel*, and when her illness left her for a time she even exceeded the quota, though this was rare. More often than not she listened to the radio, frequently singing at her sewing machine and conducting at the same time, so that the stitch went randomly. She spent the greater part of the day running to the telephone to call her mythical men. She called me, too, waking me with her early calls and babbling utter nonsense. Not infrequently our conversations would be interrupted and a woman's strange, gruff voice could be heard on the receiver: this was the foreman driving Sonya away from the telephone and back to her machine. Sonya would answer her with bad language, too.

Sometimes after work the foreman would assemble all the patients and send them off in formation on a cultural excursion to see a film. One day I saw such a group. It was comical to watch as the small queue – there were only some fifteen persons in all – stretched out farther and farther into the distance. The end ones were straggling along half a kilometre behind the ones in front. They would stop along the way, peering dully at something, and the shop foreman barely managed to collect them all in time for the show. The foreman also was probably a bit sick. She, too, had an obtuse face and she was screaming at the other patients. Sonya said that their foreman also received a disability pension, but she had only a third-class disability, the least serious kind. It was even more comical to watch these patients going to the May Day celebrations with little flags in their hands. They straggled along, straying here and there, open-mouthed and wild-eyed.

Mama was long unable to obtain sickness benefits for Sonya, although she had a second-class disability. Someone had told mama that it was possible to get eighteen roubles a month which would have been a great help to our family budget, but everyone gave her the same answer: Sonya had to work first for two years. At last, either the laws changed, or Sonya had put in her time, but in 1972 they gave her a pension, and what a pension – a whole forty roubles! True, because of these forty roubles she was continually at war with mother, since each one wanted to manage the money herself.

Sonya often went out at night and roamed for hours on end, so mama decided to keep the door key herself at night; whereupon Sonya decided to go out through the window. First she threw from our fifth-floor flat her invariable companion, the handbag, and then she got ready to go out immediately after it. It was a good thing that quite by chance mama had gone to the lavatory and had seen her in the kitchen, standing by the open window. Mama managed to lead her out of the kitchen and put her to bed. My parents slept very lightly. Mama often went in to check whether Sonya was asleep, but even so she would manage to get up and wander about the flat, poking about the saucepans and eating everything in them. Sometimes she didn't even leave the food which was intended for father in the morning and he had to go to work hungry. She left cigarette smoke all over the flat. She loved to smoke and, despite her gluttony, she wanted to lose weight and become thin.

One day she was standing flattened against the sitting-room wall, listening to something. Then she called me over, her eyes round and full of mystery, and said, 'Listen, someone's talking inside the wall.' For the sake of appearances I approached and listened for a while, telling her gravely that there was no one talking. Then she flattened herself against the wall again, suddenly exclaiming in a glad voice, 'He's heard me at last, my Robertino. It's him. He's telling me that he'll come for me soon, and he's heard my singing, and he's quite carried away. He's definitely going to marry me, and I'll sing with him in Italy!'

More and more often she heard this voice saying things to her, amorous things for the most part. It spoke to her of her beauty, saying that she was more beautiful, talented and intelligent than anyone else on earth. Sometimes Sonya would announce to us that the voice had told her that she would soon be leaving us altogether and going far, far away. She even named the exact date which the voice had mentioned to her, but the day came and she remembered nothing. She was obsessively in love with this voice and she began to believe that I was Robertino, and she would look at me with love in her eyes and embrace me passionately, to a point where I became very frightened. We had a record by Robertino Loretti in the house, and Sonya listened to it endlessly. Maybe his voice, which was very beautiful, had brought her to such a state. It was very painful for all of us to see her in such a condition, and, speaking frankly, even to live with her, and my parents returned her to the hospital. But her imaginary love of Robertino Loretti continued for several years and assumed some fantastic forms.

When I was already living with my husband, Sonya came to see us and related how as she was walking down a certain street, she saw a young fellow hopelessly drunk. He could hardly walk and was stumbling all over. Sonya began to feel very sorry for him and decided to help him by taking him home. She did this eagerly and in all sincerity, taking his arm and leading him. Along the way she asked him his name: he was called Vitya.

Sonya looked him in the eyes and said earnestly, 'No, that's not true. You're not Vitya, you're Robertino.'

Then he said, looking down modestly, 'Yes, I'm Robertino Loretti.'

They went to the Italian embassy. Vitya – that is to say, Robertino – invited her into the embassy, but Sonya said that she was 'not properly dressed'. And all the while she spoke with such conviction that one wanted to believe her, although my husband still attempted with pettifogging pedantry to refute her by pointing out that the Italian embassy was not on the street where she was supposed to have been walking; but Sonya explained that she had mixed up the streets. She seemed to like the word 'embassy', uttering it with great significance.

She was very proud that she had a sister like myself, and also that I was an artist and my husband a writer; she liked mentioning this when she met people. At the same time she used to tell us fantastic stories about her imaginary men and her adventures with them. She sincerely believed in these fictions, although sometimes she very likely realized that they were indeed fictions. She was always the first to find the men with whom she fell in love, and it was she who arranged the meetings with them. For some reason she arranged these meetings outside the lavatory on Smolensk Square. When she walked down the street, she always felt that all the men were looking at her and falling in love with her.

Because she was in love, she suddenly began to write poems to Robertino Loretti and she used to bring them to us to show to my husband, asking him to be sure to publish them in Italy. She implored him to do this, at the same time frightening him with her huge body and flailing arms. He agreed to publish them in Italy simply to pacify her and each time she came to us with new poems she asked him whether her poems had been published there. My husband would nod his head fervently in confirmation and then she would throw up her eyes dreamily and say that now her Robertino would see from her poems that she loved him. An amusing incident occurred in connection with these poems and Sonya's habit of going up to strange men. After the mathematician and poet Aleksandr Yesenin-Volpin had been placed in a mental hospital because of his protests in defence of human rights, a very large woman with an oriental face came up to him during a stroll, being attracted by his beard and learned appearance. She told him that she was a poet and that her poetry was being published in Italy. Yesenin-Volpin replied seriously that he, too, was a poet, but that his poetry was published in America. He asked how she had got herself printed in Italy, to which she replied, 'My brother-in-law Amalrik helped me. I'm going to leave hospital quite soon and go to Italy.' He smiled at this and told her that if she went on talking like that, she would hardly be getting out of there soon. After leaving hospital, Yesenin-Volpin, who had heard about my husband, told his friends with amazement about this encounter. Although my sister of course never went to Italy, Yesenin-Volpin himself left for the USA in 1971.

Sonya was not content with just poetry, so she decided to write a book about her life, beginning with early childhood. She immediately told my husband and me of her decision, to which he replied that it would probably be something like Lev Tolstoy's *Childhood, Adolescence and Youth*. 'Yes! Yes!' said Sonya excitedly, although she had never read a word of Tolstoy; and from that time on she always called her future book *Childhood, Adolescence and Adventures*; either she had simply forgotten the word 'youth' – this often happens to her – or else she wanted her title to be somewhat different from Tolstoy's. We did not think she would write so much as a single line, but one day she brought us her memoirs which were, as it happens, short enough for me to cite here in their entirety:

> It was a bright summer day: the sun was shining and children were playing in the yard. It was twelve o'clock noon on the 7th of July and my mother was giving birth to me. My childhood was unhappy. I saw no happiness in my childhood. One day my father came home drunk and threw a galosh at my mother. Father beat us a lot when we were children. He often drank and we lived in an old house, in a room of twelve square metres: four children, mother and father – six persons in all. It was crowded; we slept on the floor.
>
> I have an elder sister. She was a poor pupil and completed only five years' schooling, but she had artistic talent. She drew well and she had a teacher, a good artist. She had many friends. She grew up and became very, very pretty. Lots of men fell in love with her. She was tall and slender, with eyes like coals.
>
> But one day I was out of the house and when I returned home, I didn't find her in: she had run away somewhere, rather far. We did not know ourselves where on earth she

was. She had taken her suitcase and rushed off without saying good-bye.

A year passed, and we got no letters the whole year, and suddenly she turns up with a suitcase in her hand, pale, distraught and thinner. Mother asked, 'Where have you been?'

'I've been in Siberia, together with Andrei!'

The manuscript breaks off here.

I must say that all of us except my youngest sister have a desire to write, or more precisely, a certain need to do so: perhaps this is our great-grandfather's blood coming out in us. Sonya and Mansur are undoubtedly talented by nature, but they grew up in unpromising surroundings, with a total lack of understanding on the part of our parents and school, and in an atmosphere of general indifference altogether. None of their early promise was able to be channelled into creative work and with no outlet or freedom it took the form solely of that terrible illness, schizophrenia. I am very sorry about my brother who went mad before my very eyes not long ago, at a time when Sonya had long been ill, thus making an already strained situation extra tense. The atmosphere in our home was indeed extremely strained: everyone was short-tempered and so aggressive that the whole family could have been put away. Perhaps my parents contributed to the progression of the illness in Sonya and Mansur. My parents never spoke calmly and evenly, but always in an abusive, commanding tone; or else they simply expressed themselves by beating us. Consequently, if one of us children did anything wrong, no one would own up to it to our parents. Moreover, the guilty one would not even admit it to himself, but would put the blame on others, thereby excusing himself, as it were. I remember that owing to my fear of being beaten by my parents, a feeling gradually grew in me that I was never guilty of anything; but at the same time I developed a strong sense of resentment and alienation. It was the same with the other children.

Walks

As a child I loved going out walking by myself in the direction of the embankment. It was quite near our house, behind the house in which I had lived as a baby and in the basement of which I had seen the terrible ceiling-high woman. There was a high fence with a hole through which I crawled, then I ran across the tram line and emerged on to the Moscow River embankment. Next to the house stood long wooden barracks, out of which soldiers were always pouring, and beyond the barracks and the house there opened out the broad, sandy, perpetually sunny embankment. One could walk right up to the water. I loved it most of all when enormous barges with their little houses and cargo machinery passed down the river. They moved terribly slowly, infinitely slowly, and to me each one was an entire floating island, a floating world. The steamer horns would hoot and howl, cutting the air. I felt – and maybe it really was true – that at the sound of the horn my hair rose together with my body, as if I were taking wing. The waves rushed towards me. I felt that they were carrying me along with them into the unknown and I clutched the beautiful pebbles which the waves had left me. I loved gathering these pebbles. I often found stone fingers on the sand. When we were together, my girlfriends said that these stones were the devil's fingers. They did indeed resemble a sharply pointed finger and one could even stick one's own finger inside them a little. My girlfriends always tried to frighten me by saying that the devil would see his fingers on my fingers and take me away. I was a little uneasy, but I did not want to give them up. I was interested to see what would happen, but nothing did happen and I was no longer afraid. I still don't know what kind of stones they were; there were lots of them on the sand.

There were also lots of different bashful snails on the sand; they hid when you took them in your hand. Near the soldiers' barracks there were very deep foundation diggings, some four metres in depth and flooded with water. Reeds and flowers grew out of the water. The walls of the diggings were overgrown with dense grass. I often bathed there and chased after strange dragonflies and butterflies. I always spent a lot of time there, as far as possible from our yard and the nasty little boys. In the evenings near the barracks there were always soldiers and women sitting together. I recall that these women, who had red faces and hands, often used to sit with their arms around the soldiers, cracking sunflower seeds at the same time. Very often they danced and sang humorous verses. One evening when it was already quite dark, I was walking by the diggings and decided to go down to the water, and I looked – and there, floating on the water below, were the white bodies of babies. They were dead. I felt frightened and went home quickly. This was the time when abortions were banned.

As my youngest sister Khalida, or Galya, began to grow up, developing into a beautiful little girl (she was especially beautiful at three to four years), she was my pride. She was curly-headed, with very light hair and dark eyes, like cherries. Her face was fair, clear and sweet. I proudly took her for walks and passers-by often turned round to look at her, some even offering sweets. I was awfully fond of showing her off to everybody. In contrast to her beauty, there was my ugly appearance: my swarthy face, very bandy legs and frightened eyes. I looked as though something was crushing or falling on me. When I leaned my head to one side, I was an extremely sorry sight. Passers-by often asked who my sister was – she was so pretty – and I would answer with joy and pride that she was my sister. Sometimes they did not believe it. As a child I never looked at myself in the mirror, but one day someone took a picture of us little girls in the yard. I saw myself in the photograph and was horrified. I was ready to cry and from then on I considered myself ugly and felt ugly. As a result of the way I felt, everyone else felt that I was ugly. Later on, I am glad to say, I freed myself from this oppressive feeling.

I used to go with my beautiful sister Galya to the Schmidtovsky children's park. There was every possible game there, lots of swings and even an open theatre where the Pioneers often performed; they put on children's plays and sang children's songs. There was a large swimming pool, but one had to pay to use it. I think it was one rouble an hour (ten kopecks in present-day money). With its various amusements the children's park was the most interesting thing we had when we were young. It took the place of our mama and papa and we felt drawn there because we did not have a single toy at home. Nor was there anything interesting for me in the yard. So I often went, either alone or with my sisters, to the park or to the diggings on the embankment where I could swim and catch butterflies.

Tatar and Russian holidays

I especially remember Tatar holidays because they differ rather sharply from Russian holidays by virtue of their religious and traditional character. I have not particularly studied the meaning of each holiday, so I shall talk about them in a general way, as I saw them as a child. I shall tell about our big holiday, the Great Fast, which occurs in March. One has to fast a whole month then, from dawn to dusk. The rest of the time one can eat, but one cannot drink alcohol. The men would go to the mosque to pray, but women cannot go into the mosque. Only the old women can go inside while the young women stand in the courtyard of the mosque and also pray. We children were not taken to the mosque, because it was difficult to get in. It was surrounded by militia to keep order and the Muslims would enter the mosque in a long queue. After they had prayed, they would come out, making room for others. Muslims take off their shoes at the door. All this I heard from my parents, but I never saw the mosque as a child: I imagined it from what my parents told me. My parents wanted to take me there after I had grown up. During this holiday young people met at the mosque in their best clothes. They went there to see one another and to show themselves, as they say, so I doubt that they went out of religious feelings. When my parents returned, the first thing on their lips was a description of the people there: who was wearing what, and which relatives they had met. They brought back heaps of gossip and that is why I didn't want to go there, to a bride-show, as it were. I first saw the mosque as late as 1972. I had long been married and went there with mama.

My parents were often asked why they did not bring their eldest daughter who was old enough to be shown and to meet young men; but this did not interest me. In my youth I feared and disliked crowds. Moreover, I was unsure of myself, as I have already said. I think that generally speaking, Tatar young people are indifferent to religion: what remains is not faith in God, but only the cult of God. Young people went to the mosque as if to a show; there was nothing else in Moscow for Tatar young people: no Tatar theatre, no newspaper or club, and the mosque was the only centre for the small Tatar colony, which kept itself apart from the Russians.

Throughout the Great Fast Tatars were supposed to invite guests in the evenings. When we had lots of guests I tried to get out of the house to avoid idle questions: I know that guests often pretend to be interested in their host's children. The most important guest of all I reckoned to be my first cousin once removed. He was very swaggering and really did look very important. He resembled a solid businessman: tall, stout and handsome. I always felt that when he was talking with someone, he was listening more to his own voice than to that of the other person. He admired himself, his own words and the rounded gestures of his soft hands. He seemed to round off everything around him, and with his large, expressive eyes he took in everything. He had the sentimentality of a poet when he talked with women and many women liked him, although he was married and had heaps of children. The rest of the family held him in respect: first, because he was rich; second, because he was a very tactful and charming man. I felt there was something artistic and well-formed in him. I loved him more than the other guests; I could talk with him about my ancestors and the Tatar poets. He liked Abdullah Tukai very much and considered him Pushkin's equal.

Although I had a secret belief in some higher spirit, I had not the slightest desire to go anywhere near a mosque to surrender myself wholly to God in my prayers. I do this anywhere when I am alone with myself, so the mechanical process of prayer itself is quite unnecessary. The result is, in my opinion, really a bit theatrical: half of your prayers go into senseless gestures and not to God. Later on I developed a strange interest and attraction to the Russian Church, its icons and, particularly, church singing. I remember once I was in church with my teacher, an artist, and he looked at me and said that being in church became me; for some reason he imagined me as a meek little girl with a candle in my hand. I was very moved by the choir and the enormous hall, the walls of which were hung with magnificent icons; and there were candles burning all round as if betokening something bright and supreme. I felt here a divine emotion within me and my body trembled as though it wanted to soar and I began to weep because of the way I felt. In that Russian church I became firmly convinced of my faith in God and in the martyr Jesus. I found him right there in that Russian church. I was amazed myself by my discovery and was very grateful to my teacher for having taken me to church. But at home I always laughed at my parents. I laughed at their alleged belief in God; indeed, at the time they were doing the sort of things which a real believer would not have done. When I exposed them, it always made them very angry, especially my father. I also remember that when I was seventeen I asked my mama why she had had a lot of abortions: after all, it is a sin to kill a living being. To which mama replied with a sigh, 'If you knew what life was about, you wouldn't say such things to me,' and she wouldn't speak to me for a long time afterwards. Of course, I would not say such things to mama now.

I want to say something about the Tatar weddings which I attended as a child. Usually when there is a wedding there are always a great many people, and you wonder where so many Tatars have come from, and usually each couple that have been invited to the wedding also bring their children. The children all get acquainted under the table because there is no room for small children around the table. They play their games there, under the table. Indeed, I remember how I once came to find myself under the table. I wanted awfully much to see the bride: after all, brides are supposed to be very beautiful, like *peris*, or so I thought as a child. I was sitting on mama's knees, my eyes dazzled by the abundance of various dishes. I wanted to sample them all, but everyone was waiting for the bride and groom. Everyone was talking about them, showering fervent praise on him and her and there was excitement, movement and jovial exclamations around the table, and finally the bride and groom appeared. I was astonished when I saw the homely, long-nosed bride, and I said loudly to mama, 'What kind of bride is this? She doesn't look like a bride, she looks like a witch!' Mama leapt from her chair in surprise and then began spluttering at me, sending me back under the table as punishment. So I was unable to sample all the food on the table; I could only listen under the table to how the wedding was going. I could hear someone singing refrains for the groom, cleverly composing panegyrics out of hand as he stood there. Then a singer with a plate in his hand walked around in a circle, singing the same song. There were two goblets on the plate, one for the bride and one for the groom. The singer collected money from everybody, each person putting his donation on the plate. First they put some by the groom's goblet. I must say, everyone tried to show that he was no poorer than the next man, each person casting sidelong glances to see how much his or her neighbour gave. I understood this better on the way home when my parents told a close relative of ours that we had given no less than the others, although we were poor; later they recalled who had put what on the plate. For some reason I felt very unpleasant listening to this: it was such a mean-spirited conversation. When the singer has finally made the rounds and collected money for the groom, he pours some wine into the groom's goblet and at the same time, in the name of all the guests, sings praise and glory to the groom. Then the singer goes around again, this time collecting for the bride, and he sings a panegyric to her, too. I crawled out from under the table and looked at the big-nosed bride and the rather handsome groom: they were standing with their heads bowed modestly. The singer was pouring wine into the bride's goblet, and the bride and groom kissed in front of the guests; then each drained a goblet, and all the guests cried, 'Drink it up! Drink it up!' Then all the guests sang songs in unison. It was beautiful. I should mention that besides money the guests also brought a great number of gifts: clothing, pillows, bed linen, quilts, dishes, plates and a wall clock, and all this lay piled up in another room.

Russian holidays differ from Tatar holidays in that they have lost, if not their traditional character, then at least their originality, their Russian spirit. There is something faceless, dreary and confused in modern holidays. Now, in place of the pre-revolutionary religious holidays there are holidays with military parades, long speeches and patriotic marches. People have accepted these holidays with a kind of special desperation; and if they go strolling during the holidays and spend their last kopecks on vodka and special delicacies, it is as if to say: we, too, know how to stroll, no worse than the next man. At home they throw themselves into their dancing and take their dancing and drunken songs out on to the street, as if to say: we can take a walk as well as the next man. With their drunken affability they idly accost passers-by, and their houses smell of drink, and the gramophone blares out: 'Mishka, Mishka, where is your smile?' or 'Johnny, you don't know me!' And these songs resound louder and louder from almost every window and the air is full of the smell of spirits and the sounds of the gramophone. It was simply impossible to escape from these sounds: they could be heard on all sides at home and from all the windows in the street. There was something sinister and even tragic in this.

Russians drink even when there is no holiday, each man making a holiday for himself. When I see a drunk walking along all by himself, waving his arms about and yelling out his songs, or else swearing at someone, I begin to feel sorry for him. I think: it is not because he has a good life that he is singing and swearing so violently. He is explaining to passers-by that he loves his Russia and that he is a patriot, but that he is not on the Communists' side, because they do everything badly; because no matter how hard he works, he will still not have enough money to provide for his family, and even if his wife also works, they will still not have enough to make both ends meet; because there is nowhere for him to chat, not even with a friend. In his room he has a wife and children, and you can't have a heart-to-heart talk very well in the street either – indeed, there is now nowhere to sit and have even a glass of beer and talk and talk and unburden one's Russian soul. Try to talk just a little bit louder, try to unbosom your soul, and you'll get yourself into prison because of that nice soul of yours. But with whom can you have a heart-to-heart talk at home: with your wife, who has worries of her own? Indeed, after work, what with the children and all kinds of housework, a wife even forgets that she has a husband. So where can you get the kind of attention you need if a woman is so overworked that she has not even a moment to look after herself? So this drunken husband of hers is walking along in quite the opposite direction to his own home after drinking away all his money. He does not want to hear her reproaches each and every time.

The revolutionary holidays depressed rather than gladdened me. During holidays I wanted only one thing: to fall asleep for the duration of each holiday and then to wake up later and quietly rejoice at each new day.

My hatred of school

I had a bad time at school. I used to listen to the teacher very inattentively and absent-mindedly, and consequently I often did not know what she was talking about or what she wanted. I had an especially hard time with arithmetic. I would move the various ciphers about senselessly, producing the most fantastic solutions, so that when checking them afterwards my teacher in her anger would mark a 'one' across the whole paper. However, the most agonizing thing for me was when I was called to the blackboard and the whole class, or so it seemed, was watching me. There could be no question of my solving on the blackboard a problem which I was unable to solve even in my exercise book. I puffed and panted, making no headway, writing and erasing all the while; and once I so strained myself in my unrealizable desire to solve a problem that my elastic broke and my knickers came off. Everything went misty before my eyes – I was so ashamed – but I did manage to look at the class and it appeared that no one had noticed anything. So I pulled out my knickers from under my feet and began to erase the ill-starred problem from the blackboard with them, as though they were a rag. Generally speaking, I was a terrible scatterbrain, sometimes losing my shabby clothes, sometimes my exercise books, sometimes my money. Once when my parents sent me to the store I lost a hundred roubles (ten in present-day money). This was considered very big money at the time: one could live thriftily for several days on it. I was too frightened to go home and spent half a day crying outside the store.

I recall that for some reason my teacher loved to seat her pet honours pupils in the first rows and in the first seats, whereas poor, inattentive pupils sat at the hindmost benches, so the teacher would not even have to see them. This made it all the more difficult for these pupils to see and hear, but as it happened I liked sitting at the back so as not to be in the teacher's field of vision. There I could draw or read stories behind the other pupils' backs. I went to a girls' school up to the third form. This school was located near Smolensk Square in a side-street with clanging trams. I used to ride to school on the tram, a distance of several stops. In the autumn of 1954, when they started mixing the girls and the boys, I was sent to another school nearer my home, a five-minute walk. Of course, the boys introduced into the classroom a certain disorder and noise – anarchy, in short – but, to tell the truth, they also brought a certain amount of variety and freshness. The girls were generally of little interest as I recall: they were strongly under the teacher's influence. The honours pupils acted primly, toadying to the teacher, and they were all nothing but tell-tales. But the boys had an element of fantasy and contradiction and they hardly ever told tales.

One day a new girl turned up in our class, having moved to Moscow from another town. The girl was unusually quiet and unassuming: I have already forgotten her name. She was not exactly a bad pupil, but not a good one either: sometimes she even received 'twos'. But I remember that she never cried, but just bit her lips till they bled and stared straight ahead. She was swarthy, with sad, dark eyes. For some reason I liked her very much, but she did not make friends with anyone and kept apart from the others. This made many of us curious and interested in her. She was nicknamed 'the pilgrim' after one day in physical education class one of the girls noticed a tiny cross on a thin chain around her neck. The teacher heard about this at once: a gaggle of girls and boys had gathered round the teacher straight away and whispered something to her mysteriously. She sent them all out of the room and went up to the girl. I heard their conversation because I was being punished for something, perhaps for not finishing an assignment, and I had to stay in the room. I heard the teacher ask her whether she believed in God and whether she wanted to become a Pioneer: after all, if she went on believing in God and wearing a cross around her neck they wouldn't take her into the Pioneers. She would be unworthy of wearing their tie. 'For shame!' the teacher exclaimed, and then said that she was going to meet with her parents. The girl made no reply to all this but only pressed her lips together hard and hung her head. From that moment she became mysterious and altogether inaccessible to me. I felt respect and an invisible kinship with her. True, after her talk with the teacher she ceased to wear her cross in class. She attended my school for only a year, unfortunately, and then disappeared just as unexpectedly as she had arrived.

I was accepted into the Pioneers in the fourth form. Although I was a bad pupil, our class had pledged that in the new year there would be no non-Pioneers. We all had to be Pioneers and I was pushed into the organization. I recall that I was very afraid of becoming a Pioneer. When it happened my parents would not even let me in the house although my teacher had inducted me by force, as it were, and against my wishes. I was even bought a tie from public funds: they had found a cheap cotton one somewhere. Before receiving us into the Pioneers – we were all the very worst pupils in class and were being taken into the Pioneers at the end of the queue – we were given the 'oath of Lenin' to learn. Long and very boring, it consisted in my promising to be a good pupil, to help younger children, to love Lenin and Stalin wholeheartedly, to obtain only 'fours' and 'fives', and a great number of other long promises which I simply cannot remember.

Then, after we had made these promises, the Pioneer leader raised her hand to her temples and declared, 'Pioneers, be prepared for the struggle for the cause of Lenin and Stalin!'

We slow learners were all supposed to have learned the reply: 'Ever prepared!' And so they hung our ties on us. I felt strange and awkward having this tie on me.

In class the teacher said proudly, 'Now our class is first: we're all Pioneers.'

On the way home I hid my tie in my bag and said nothing to my parents about being accepted into the Pioneers; it was only perhaps a year later that my parents found out. Father was especially angry. He told me that I was an atheist now that I had become a Pioneer, and that this would cost me dearly, and that I had exchanged Allah the Most High for this tie, this red rag; and he tore up the tie. It made no difference to me, but I was unable to prove to him that I would not have been able to go to school otherwise and that I myself did not want to be a Pioneer. But father would not listen to anything and just shouted and shouted.

But even though I had become a Pioneer, I was as poor a pupil as I had been before my induction. Such a high calling as that of Pioneer had not helped me to improve in my studies after all and I repeated almost every class. Later, I became utterly bored with going to school: I reckoned that I was only wasting valuable time, that going to school was simply not interesting, and that it would be better and more interesting for me to sit at home and draw or look at the green wallpaper and try to make out the invisible shapes of fairy-tale forms. Every year it became harder and harder for me to endure school. I began to grow up, and with age – and apparently even as early as childhood – my imperceptibly developing feeling of my own inferiority grew sharper and sharper. I was ashamed of my appearance, my ugliness, my height, my long legs and arms and sharp elbows. I was ashamed of my nationality, and although I did not want to be Russian, I was still ashamed of what I felt to be a Tatar primitiveness and lack of culture.

Friends

One day I was racking my miserable brains over an arithmetic problem. There was no way I was going to be able to solve it myself – I had such a hard time with arithmetic that I concluded once and for all that I was a dunce, and sometimes the teacher, sometimes the other pupils, and sometimes the other girls in my building would try to help me with it – so I decided to run downstairs to ask one of the girls for help. As luck would have it, the girls whom I usually asked to help me were out, and in panic – it was already time to go to school, and I still had an unsolved problem – I remembered that downstairs, on the first floor, there lived a girl who was three years older than I. Although I had a bad impression of her as someone who was always malicious, mocking and spiteful, always imagining herself more intelligent than the others and consequently supercilious, I went off to see her, keeping my opinion of her to myself. She happened to be at home and I was met at the door by a cat of startling dimensions. With his repulsive eyes he strangely resembled the girl herself and he kept on hissing at me at the door. (The cat was very fluffy.) I was very glad that Alya – that was her name – was at home and that she agreed to help me. After reading through the problem Alya explained the gist of it and almost literally chewed it over for me, but I remained completely uninterested in all this. She even adduced examples from real life, but before me stood nothing but bare, abstract figures, and these figures seemed a whole cosmos to me. She then simply gave me the solution to the problem, I wrote it down and, thanking her, went off to school, but the next day I was back at her place again and did my homework there. I do not know why I was drawn to her. Perhaps she was an authority figure for me, like an older friend. Perhaps I was attracted to her by the fact that she drew and showed me her drawings.

Alya had grown up without a father and lived alone with her mother. The latter was at work from morning till evening, so Alya was left by herself the whole day. She warmed up her own food and even prepared simple things for herself. She used to get bored eating alone so she often invited me to eat with her. I was always hungry of course and I recall the pleasure with which I ate her sausages and shop-made rissoles and the potatoes that she herself had fried. In this respect she was not mean, but on the whole she was a very strange girl. She always irritated me by her self-assurance and by the arrogance with which she treated me. She even talked in a know-all voice with her mother and sniffed scornfully at everything. Her face was sallow, sharp and bony and she had malicious, glowing eyes – small, like gimlets. She liked showing off in front of me. She was always arguing and loved to have the last word. I always felt that there was something dirty, unnatural and depraved about her. For example, I noticed that when she thought I was not looking she would pick her nose and put the snot into her mouth. I also noticed her bad habit of sniffing the sweat under her arms. But for me the strangest thing about her was what I shall now relate.

It was very cold outside. Autumn had arrived, there was a freezing rain, and I didn't want to go home so I decided to drop in on her. She was even glad that I had come. She asked if I was hungry and happily and readily gave me something to eat. It was very cold in the house, too, and she suggested going to bed to get warm. We took off our dresses and lay down. We started to talk about something, I can't remember what, but then she began to be curious about what my breasts were like. I felt embarrassed that she was asking me about them: my breasts appeared very late, I think only when I was about fifteen, and I was then only thirteen. She began to examine me without ceremony and then suggested that I should feel what her breasts were like. For some reason I began to feel terribly shy. She appeared strange, curious and cheeky. I decided not to touch her breasts. I was even afraid, because I was used to having no breasts myself. I thought that that was how it was supposed to be and when she said that hers were already large and kept on suggesting that I should touch them, it seemed strange to me to have bumps on a flat place. Then, seeing my awkwardness and fear, and at the same time telling me that there was nothing terrible there and calling me a coward, she took my hand and began to move it about on a soft bump. Her breasts were very large for a sixteen-year-old, and on the ends of them there were pimples, like small buttons. She moved my hands over her breasts like this for a long time. I tore my hands away in fear. She tried to make me feel ashamed about being afraid and funking a simple game or joke, with the result that I began to calm down and even yielded to her somewhat, since she was older. She moved my hand still lower, below her belly, and here I became even more frightened as I came up against something prickly, like a brush. I even screamed in surprise and fright, but she called me a fool and said that I was lily-livered; and she grabbed my hands still tighter.

So, after warming myself a while I left her. The fact that she played and joked (or so I believed) in such a way aroused no suspicion on my part, because an interest in the metamorphoses of nature is common in young boys and girls, but later I saw this episode with Alya in a somewhat different light. I realized that there was some other aspect to this, but I could not find the word for it, and it was only later that I found out what the word 'lesbian' means; and this word took me back into the past, to my childhood and this strange girl, Alya. I now recall a friend of hers the same age talking to me about her very enigmatically. This friend was called Galya. She was very plain, freckled and broad-faced, but kind and friendly. When she was on bad terms with Alya she hinted to me at her strangeness, but I did not understand then what she was talking about, merely guessing vaguely. I recalled my episode with Alya, began to feel embarrassed and changed the subject. I concluded that Alya had probably played with this Galya as she had done with me. Despite the fact that I felt towards Alya a hatred which even I did not understand, I continued to visit her and therein lay her obvious power over me. She could even laugh and scoff at me during our arithmetic lessons: I endured it all patiently.

There was a little girl named Arina in our yard. She was a

year and a half or two years my junior. Somehow I had not noticed her: she had always seemed plain and puny to me. She was very short, almost like a child, but as if to make up for it her father was in my opinion a very interesting man. He had the look of a writer or a musician, with long, raven-coloured hair brushed back, which often fell on to his temples in thick, unruly strands, and horn-rimmed glasses, and dark, piercing eyes which always looked kindly at children as he passed them. Sometimes he even took part in games, despite the fact that he was close upon fifty. He loved children and knew how to joke with them, and as he did it his dark eyes always sparkled very slyly.

Once I went up to him to ask where Arina was, and he replied, 'Ah, it's you. Come a little closer.' I approached hesitantly, whereupon he asked me, 'How long did you torment us, Tatar-mator-gubernator?!' and looked at me sternly.

I said nothing, for I had not expected such a conversation with him, or such a strange question. Then he asked me the same thing again, even more threateningly. I stood there, silent as before, and was by then almost in tears.

Then he said to me, 'Hm, you don't know, so now I'll tell you: you tormented us for three hundred years, Tatar-mator. And now tell me how many years you tormented us.'

Trembling and weeping, I repeated it, drawling it out, 'Three hundred . . .' – and at this point he began to cough terribly. It was the beginning of an asthma attack and he was in tears from the painful coughing for a long time afterwards. Meanwhile I gradually calmed down and began to feel sorry for him: he was red and all in tears. Although I had been frightened by his question, even so I was gratified to learn that at one time the Tatars had tormented the Russians and it was not only the case, as it seemed to me, that the Russians tormented the Tatars.

I dropped in on Arina occasionally. They had a harmonium and I liked to play it. The harmonium resembled an organ in miniature and looked very beautiful. I learned to play a fast chopsticks on it, ta-ta-ta ta-ta, and I also learned 'Little siskin, little deer, where have you been?' All this I played without music since I didn't know any music. I simply memorized the position of the keys by watching Arina play and then repeating it after her. Her father, Uncle Borya, was a musician. He even had his own orchestra which he had organized with the help of friends of his who were amateur musicians and with this orchestra he performed in various places. One day Arina began bragging and showed me a dog-eared newspaper – I don't remember which one – with a photograph of his orchestra. Uncle Borya was the conductor. In the photograph his horn-rimmed glasses sparkled with inspiration and behind them you could see his dark eyes, peering sharply. Such concerts afforded a poor living to the musicians and they were obliged to take other work as they could find it. Uncle Borya made his living by tuning the instruments of famous musicians and even just ordinary musicians and that is how he fed himself and his family. He died in hospital of asthma soon afterwards and I was very sorry for him. After his death it was somewhat strange not to hear his usual jokes. Arina's mother sold beer in a stall and quickly went to seed after her husband's death.

I was friends with Arina in a desultory way. She associated more with girls of her age. She laughed at me because I was friendly with such a runt. I did indeed always look down on her, but I liked being with her more than with my other friends. Arina loved music, as I did. She loved books and her father taught her to read books and to love Pushkin and Lermontov. She read avidly. What I liked about their family was that when her father was still alive, he or her mama would read a book aloud in the evenings and the others would listen. Following her family tradition, Arina loved reading books to me. One day Arina and I went to the Pushkin Museum on Volkhonka to look at pictures. Oh, how marvellous it was: this was the most fateful moment and the happiest day of my life! I believed in my happy fate and even as a child I had had a presentiment of what was later to happen. I can no longer remember what struck me more: the pictures alone, or the museum itself, together with its beautiful pictures, sculpture and painted ceilings. Everything was new to me – strange and at the same time familiar, as it were, from childhood. I thought that this was perhaps what my soul had wished for even without knowing it. I walked through the museum like a drunk person, clutching Arina's hand with my own nervous, convulsive hands. I remember that Arina often had to drag me away from a picture because she herself was already overstrained by impressions. Now I can no longer recall which pictures I saw. It was a long time ago: I was about fourteen. I do recall the general impression and the ecstasy which took hold of me. I think this powerful impression affected the whole of my subsequent destiny. I must frankly say that my friendship with this runt, as she was called, was not in vain and I am very grateful to her. Without suspecting it herself, she undoubtedly implanted in me the seeds of what I later became.

Other friends like Nadya and Tanya who were my own age did not have the same effect on me although I saw them more often. I was always almost bored with Nadya, but without her I was even more bored. Somehow it is more fun to be bored together. She and I talked about all kinds of nonsense so there is nothing to recall. We loafed about, useless to each other, and went to the shops when our mamas sent us there; and if we happened to have a few kopecks in our pockets we would buy a few toffees and walk along sucking them. I had a boring time with her, but in childhood even that was fun. We used to go sledding together and made snowmen.

It was more interesting and less monotonous to be with Tanya, the girl with whom I used to play 'hospital'. She was more lively and buoyant, a mere spring breeze, but she was also a joker and a wag. She could think up all sorts of things. She loved these various 'ideas' of hers and shared them with me, but as they were very adventurous, I was even rather afraid of them. But she knew how to stir up my enthusiasm quickly and I would yield boldly to her adventurous plans. As I have said, she was a very pretty little girl, with blue eyes, blond hair and blushing cheeks. Tanya had no difficulty in turning the boys' heads. She was also a tease. She would play jokes on some boy who had fallen in love with her and then laugh ringingly right in the embarrassed boy's face. Her jokes made them fall even more in love with her. We often went walking together. The purpose of our walks would be to meet boys or simply to show off in front of them. This was our favourite occupation and we would stroll down various avenues and boulevards; naturally we would come across similar pairs of strolling boys and some of them would follow on our heels and play pranks. If we saw that the boys were not hooligans, but quite decent boys, we would naturally show off in front of them, turning round coquettishly to make some reply; or sometimes we would pretend not to see them, and they would follow us for a long time and say things about us, discussing our figures out loud. Such boyish advances appealed to us. We were not thinking then of love or kisses: it was enough for us that we appealed to someone and were being followed. Such impressions sufficed for several days. We used to retell over and over again what one of them had said to me, and what another had said to her; we recalled all this with excitement. We also went out on dates together, but I was always a coward on dates and could find nothing to say. I always got flustered and as a result had no great success. Out of embarrassment I would often simply not keep a date. I would think about boys in the solitude of my home, but when I saw a particular boy I would want to run away and I would curse myself for my timidity and fear. Or sometimes I would simply be disappointed with a boy on a date, but at home I would endow him in my imagination with noble features. I can no longer remember all the boys I dated. I only remember that it was all unsuccessful, owing to my stupid shyness.

I liked my walks with Tanya more than school, and not only my walks with Tanya, but walks in general, even when I was alone. This was a happier time for me than going off to dreary school and seeing my rat-like teachers. School represented a most odious burden to me. I often liked to play truant and soon I decided once and for all to give up school. Tanya decided to give it up together with me and we both felt like uncaged birds. Neither her parents nor mine knew about this. We made them think that we were going to school as before and we filled in our reports with the kind of marks we wanted. We were making very good progress, at least so far as our parents knew, of course. They did not find out about this until an incident which took place under the most lamentable circumstances.

Tanya and I often dreamed of buying ourselves some sheer nylon stockings. The First of May was approaching, our parents felt that we were too young to wear sheer stockings, and we had no money. So we began to dream up ways of getting money and various plans entered our heads, each one more fantastic than the last, especially my plans. They were always devoid of reality and full of absurd fantasy.

'What if we dressed up in the most worn-out clothes we can find,' I said to her animatedly, 'and we'd look like beggars. We can go begging in such clothes. It would even be fun, like play-acting. After all, not everyone can play the part of a beggar, but we can, because I think we've got acting talent.'

But Tanya was listening to me absent-mindedly, for she was thinking up another plan at the time. She looked at me vaguely and suddenly an 'idea' dawned on her; she even gave a jump. One day I had been telling her how my sister Sonya had received in her school for mentally retarded children a little book from the Moscow Tree and Shrub-Planting Society. As I recall, since Sonya and the other pupils never went out to plant anything, the book was always lying around the house. Her first name, patronymic and surname were given, but there was no photograph. Tanya happened to think of this and she told me her brilliant 'idea': to take Sonya's book and go from house to house and flat to flat collecting money for planting courtyards as though for the purchase of saplings and seed. Clever Tanya even invented a special list. She took an exercise book, divided it into columns and gave each one a different heading: 'name of street', 'house number', 'flat number', 'surname', 'amount' and 'signature'. Before going out we decided to fill in the list a bit, inserting various surnames and amounts and adding little flourishes, so that the tenants would think that they were not the first and would not be the last. We chose beforehand the building that we would go into: it was some distance from our block so that they would not know our faces.

In the entrances to some of the blocks there were iron boards showing the tenants' surnames. From these we copied down the surnames on our list and then went from flat to flat collecting money. We even put on our Pioneer ties as an added precaution. The tenants of the flats received us politely and even praised us for our good Pioneer work, saying that now, finally, they had thought of useful work and the courtyard was going to be green, for they were sick of it as it was with only worthless boys running around beneath their windows breaking them with their balls. So they told us their grievances and gave what they could afford and we held out our exercise book and asked them to sign it. One man who opened the door to us was a military man. He questioned us for a long time as to what sort of a society this was and what school we went to. We repeated what we had agreed on at home, but he began to have doubts, said he had no money and slammed the door. Some of the other tenants also regarded our undertaking with distrust so we waved our little book casually in front of them. The little book usually produced results, although no one examined it closely; but they did not always give money. In this way we collected what we regarded as a great deal of money: some twenty roubles. We wanted to continue our collection in another block, but, overjoyed, we started counting the money right there before we had left the doorway, when all of a sudden the man in the military uniform came down the stairs. He approached us resolutely and asked if we had collected a lot. We froze on the spot and stood there indecisively muttering something in repy whereupon he said that we were not to leave and that when someone else came along he would tell him to ring the militia.

Before we could collect ourselves, two militiamen grabbed us and led us off to the militia station. Along the way I thought feverishly about how to get rid of the list which lay in my pocket. As it happened I had a hole in my pocket and I wanted to get rid of it through the hole, but one of the militiamen was walking behind us and he would see me drop it. At the very last moment, seeing that we were approaching the station, in despair I finally dropped the ill-starred list, but the militiaman walking along behind picked it up, saying, 'Hey, you, don't discard anything,' and handed me the list. We entered a long, narrow corridor which was very dark despite the fact that it was daytime and there were two windows; but light penetrated there reluctantly. Along the walls stood tables with ink pots and penholders with clumsy pens. The sergeant left us after telling a colleague who was walking back and forth behind a barrier to keep an eye on Tanya and me while he himself went into the chief's office to make his report on us. Some time later he came out of the office with a sheet of paper in his hand. He sat down and gave each of us a form so that we could write down what had motivated us to do what we had done, and why, as well as where we went to school, where we lived and whether we had parents. We sat there for a long time not knowing what to do. I was afraid that she would write something that might hurt me. She wrote nothing either and was afraid that I would write the wrong thing. We tried to look each other in the eyes, making signs so that the militiaman would not notice and talking with our fingers the way mutes do. In this way we agreed to write nothing and we sat there awaiting our fate.

When they brought us into the station it was about two o'clock in the afternoon. We had already sat there several hours and all the callers who were there on passport business had departed, leaving only Tanya, me and the militiaman who had relieved the first one. Instead of the chief, the duty officer summoned us and said that we should write and then they would let us go home. It was by then nine o'clock in the evening and our parents were undoubtedly alarmed and in a state of panic, searching for us everywhere, while there we were in so terrible and unexpected a place. But eleven o'clock and twelve o'clock passed and we were still sitting at the table in front of the empty questionnaire. Tanya moved over to join me and the militiaman said nothing. Maybe he even felt sorry for us, because he glanced at us rather compassionately from time to time and kept asking us what our parents were doing now and what had we done to be sitting here. We were glad of such kind sympathy and with faint voices asked him to let us go, because our parents were searching all over for us and we were hungry and sleepy. But he only spread his arms and with pity in his voice said that he had been ordered not to let us go until the chief authorized it. We despaired completely and fell silent, each of us thinking about herself and weeping. After we had become quite exhausted, we leaned our heads on each other's shoulder and tried to fall asleep, even managing to nap a little. When we woke up we again saw the dim light of the electric lamp and the militiaman yawning his head off. We felt miserable and lonely and wanted our parents to find us. The hands on the wall-clock which resembled the lid of a small coffin were already approaching one o'clock in the morning.

I was overcome with a strange torpor, an indifference to anything that might happen. It was the kind of state where you seem not to exist and become part of the corridor or the clock. Everything in you buzzes and rings like a clock. The militiaman was already changing from a man into a frozen object, a still life.

But suddenly, somewhere in the direction of the entrance, bells began to ring, forcing us to rouse ourselves and emerge from our torpor. We could hear emotional female voices and the voice of the militiaman. We had already sensed something familiar in those distant voices and at last Tanya's and my own long awaited mama appeared. As soon as they saw us they immediately burst into tears. Then they began to ask us how we came to be here, but we were too excited to be able to say anything. Then they talked things over with the sergeant and went into the station chief's office. Then each of us was sent for in turn and questioned as to the whys and wherefores. I felt much better with my mama sitting in the office with us. I was not afraid for I felt that she was a kind of protection. For some reason my mama mostly answered for me although the questions were directed at me. The chief asked why I needed the money and I answered simply that I needed sheer stockings and I also wanted to buy a theatre ticket, but I had no money, so Tanya and I had thought up this idea. He asked which of us had thought it up. I was silent for a long time and then I said that we had thought it up together. He gave me a sly look and said nothing more. He wrote something and then asked why I had left school. Mama was quite surprised at this for I had been keeping it from her. Then he said that shortly – to be precise, within two weeks – I had to go back to school or else go to work, and with that he released me. I should add that the chief was a handsome, good-natured man of about fifty with grey hair. Looking at him, I was not afraid of being in his office.

First love

The militia chief had said that when after two weeks I had either got a job or was back in school, I should immediately bring him a certificate showing that I was not a parasite, but was participating in active life. Although I was a minor and could not be given a job, I did not want to go to school, and anyway my parents reckoned that it was time I was earning money so I began feverishly to look for work. But no one would take me on anywhere, saying that I was a minor. Then I went to the district executive committee to see if they would give me some kind of work, but they didn't give me any either although they did suggest that I should enter vocational school in order to learn some kind of trade, I can't remember which; but when they told me this, I refused point-blank. I saw how the vocational students went about in a special, awful uniform consisting of very unattractive clothes: the girls, in black cotton dresses with some kind of tabs, and in winter a black greatcoat of the very poorest material, also with tabs on the collar, and a black cap trimmed with the cheapest grey fur. I decided to look for something else, provided it was not vocational school.

Frankly, my own clothes were not much better, if not indeed worse, than those of the vocational students. I had no winter coat and therefore I went about in winter, autumn and spring in one and the same coat. Mama had once bought me a dark-brown coat which I had to wear for as long as possible – five years at the very least. It was unbelievably long and wide. I always tucked up the sleeves and tied it round with a belt so that it would not look so wide. All the same I looked ridiculous, as if I was going into the forest to cut firewood. The coat hung on me as if it were on a stick. I was unbelievably thin and at that time I always stooped, being ashamed of my height. Dresses – and my dresses were only cotton print – mama bought for me in too large a size as well, in case the dress should suddenly shrink after washing, or lest I outgrow it; but after a while I would secretly shorten my dresses. Footwear mama also tried to buy for me one size too large, 'to grow into', as she said; meanwhile she used to put wadding in my boots to stop them from coming off my feet. While I was wearing my boots in they looked like galoshes and were so loose they did indeed come off my feet and I was always flapping about in them.

When I went out looking for work I had no idea where I was going. I followed my nose, not wishing to go home to hear bitter reproaches about how I was neither working nor studying, but was simply eating bread which I hadn't earned. I roamed like that for days on end. I went into every institution, workshop and factory, but all without success: they did not take minors even as apprentices. I thought: it was really good before, when there were private businesses and private shops. Before, one could certainly became an apprentice in any business, but now you need certificates properly stamped. One day I went into a pharmacy to buy some medicine for mama and I surprised myself by asking the shop assistant if they had any work for me. She told me to go to see the manager. I felt that maybe here by chance I would be successful. I asked the manager whether there was any work for me and to my great joy she suggested that I might become a trainee packer, bottling medicines and packing tablets and powders in special boxes. True, they paid very little, but I was delighted that I would finally have money of my own which I myself had earned. Now my parents would not be able to reproach me with eating bread I hadn't worked for.

I did not need a lot of documents for the pharmacy, only one from the house management saying that I lived in Moscow and giving my full address, and I began work the very next day in the pharmaceutical section. Everything was white and clean and smelled of medicine. There were various flasks on the tables and mortars for making powders. I found this very interesting. The manager took me over to a woman sitting at a table in a white smock and cap and asked her to show me what to do and then went away. The woman in the white smock was very fat. Without even asking my name she told me straight away to write names on boxes and to paste labels on various phials. The work did not seem bad to me: it wasn't hard and it wasn't dirty. Then I was given medicines to bottle. I liked doing that; I liked the pharmaceutical exactness and the fact that, as I reflected, I was bottling medicines here which some sick person would be taking later. But I had not worked at the pharmacy for even two months before they started to cut back the staff and I was one of those cut back. On the whole it was old employees who stayed and I was discharged on grounds of redundancy.

Tanya and I completely lost contact after our adventure. Her parents had forbidden her to be friends with me and it was impossible to drop in to see her although she herself came to see me, but much less often than before. She was afraid that for the first few days the militia would be watching us to see whether we were going about together; in any case, that is what she told me. I did not think they would do that: after all, they had enough work without us. The militia felt easy after I got a job and Tanya also got a job in a commission shop, with the help of an aunt who was a trainee. One day Tanya came to see me and said very seriously that we should go to evening school, that we should finish school, and that she wanted to study mathematics in university. She convinced me and we went to a school for young working people not far from us. They admitted her readily, but they did not want to admit me because at the time I was no longer working; but I told the director that I was going to get a job quite soon, in a matter of days, and that I would bring a certificate, so she finally decided to let me attend the school. The very first day in class she asked who did not have a work certificate. Again I did not have one so I promised to bring one later, but I never brought one because I was utterly unable to find a job, so they forgot about me and stopped asking about the certificate.

I was in class six in this school, but I did not attend it for very long, no more than half a year. Again, I did not like the teacher, nor did I like my classmates who were coarse, working-class people. The men and boys always swore obscenely and showed no restraint in their behaviour towards the girls. It was difficult to study in such a class. As before, I was totally unable to do mathematics. Because of this I was all the more unwilling to continue my studies although I liked Russian very much. Despite the fact that this was a school for adults, the teachers conducted classes in a very dry and uninteresting way. To understand you had to listen, but when you listened you heard a monotonous voice and bookish words. I became unintentionally distracted and used to make sketches of my classmates. It is difficult for emotional natures like mine to assimilate this kind of teaching; it is difficult for us to concentrate on any one thing.

I concentrated all my attention on history class, but I got nothing but 'twos'. History was taught by a very handsome young man – tall, with luxuriant yellow hair combed straight back, blue eyes and beautiful teeth. He reminded me of a Scandinavian. He wore a velvet jacket and was full of mystery. He taught with a somewhat embarrassed expression on his face and his cheeks blushed slightly whenever he addressed a girl, but when he explained or recounted anything his face was very calm, pale and inspired. I used to watch him, all eyes, from behind my classmates' backs and with each lesson I fell more in love with him Everything he said went in one ear and out the other and I blushed terribly whenever he caught my passionate gaze. I used to be embarrassed to the point of tears and would just hang my head. Whenever he called upon me to repeat the lesson, I would reply from my desk – too embarrassed to raise my head – saying that I did not know the lesson. When he called me up to the blackboard, I would be so terribly nervous about finding myself next to him that I forgot everything I knew and he would give me a bad mark; but more often than not he would give me simply a dot which meant that I would have to repeat the lesson next time. He thus gave me many dots, but later on he began to give 'twos', though I managed to get out of the 'two' category when we had test papers. He would give us questions on sheets of paper and we were supposed to answer them. Then I received not 'twos', but 'threes' and 'fours', so I made good use of those occasions.

But I became utterly devastated and lost all interest in my studies when I inadvertently noticed a wedding ring on my teacher's finger. Previously, I had secretly hoped that he would perhaps pay some attention to me; now it became too painful to attend his classes. But suddenly my history teacher was replaced by an elderly woman and then I started attending history class again. I could not understand where he had disappeared to: had he resigned? had he been dismissed? I was sorry that he was no longer at the school. For a long time afterwards I was tormented by my love for him. I hoped that he would perhaps turn up again, but he never did. My wounds bled profusely and it felt as if someone had sprinkled salt on them as well, and these wounds stung my soul, ate up my brains and clouded my eyes. 'My love! My love! I shall die with you!' But two months passed, and I began to calm down, and my wounds skinned over a bit. I was sixteen at the time.

The beginning of my art studies

I was standing in our yard with four other girls, propping up the fence and shelling sunflower seeds out of boredom. We had nothing else to do at the time so we just watched the passers-by. I had a feeling of complete hopelessness and aimlessness then. I had not so much as an idea in my head – merely a haze and total blackness. I felt indifferent about the girls with whom I was standing, the more so as they usually went around in pairs and I was the odd one out and, as it were, superfluous and unwanted; and consequently amongst my friends I had the least say, or at best a faint echo. So I was shelling sunflower seeds and absent-mindedly watching passers-by. These were over-anxious people with briefcases and fat shopping bags, or simply bundles wrapped in newspaper. They were fat, thin, or wiry. They were all walking quickly, while their faces reflected an utter indifference to everything around them. They were going somewhere purposefully, their God only knew where. There was a kind of fanaticism or somnambulism in this. . . . And all of a sudden my attention was caught by such a sight that it would have been difficult to say what it was or who it was, but to me it was a wonder sent from heaven, or maybe even from hell. Passing by us was a middle-aged man with a thick black beard, sideburns and black curly hair combed back and reaching almost to his shoulders. He was walking very swiftly, casting an alert eye on everything around him. He was whistling something softly and delicately like a sparrow. He was unusually dressed, too, in narrow jeans which fitted closely to his strong, slim legs and a great number of jangling keys protruded from his pockets. He was also wearing a red tennis shirt full of holes which made him look like a pirate. Through his tennis shirt one could sense the moulded, bronzed body of a yogi. All this I appraised in a single second, taking it in at a glance. I was excited by this man and amazed as well. I could not help pointing to him and saying loudly, 'Girls, girls, look: it's a Neanderthal man!' The girls all turned, amazed perhaps by my uncharacteristically loud voice and unusual intonation. They immediately burst out laughing as they looked at him and we followed him with five pairs of eyes. But what was he doing? He entered our yard and headed for our entry-way. I was actually frightened, thinking that perhaps he had heard me call him a Neanderthal man and that he was going to do something now. My heart was pounding. He passed into the entry-way, leaving me in a state of numbness, agitation and excitement. I felt a hundred different things at the time.

Several minutes later I told the girls that I was going to get Alya, the very same girl with whom I had that strange friendship. After leaving school I called on her very rarely since I no longer needed her help with mathematics and also because she had an awful disposition, but on this occasion I felt an intuitive desire, as it were, to call on her. Consciously or unconsciously, I fancied that she was somehow connected with this man. And when I entered her room – yes, I saw this strange Neanderthal man. I was taken aback and did not know what to say, but I managed to squeeze out a word of greeting although I felt awkward at the time. But I had not finished speaking before this strange man's voice drowned out everything else, as he exclaimed, 'Ah, this is the girl who called me a Neanderthal man. She's a real good-for-nothing, so I'm going to make her beg my pardon, and on her knees! I know: I saw her out of the corner of my eye. It was she who said it! Who is this girl?' he asked Alya. Alya said that I lived in the same house, that I was a Tatar, and that I also drew. 'Hm,' he said, 'it's good that she draws. And what's your name?' I was called Roza. Everyone in the yard called me that, rechristening me with a Russian name, although my Tatar name is Guzel. Hearing the name 'Roza', he frowned and said, 'What a vulgar name! But what are you called in Tatar?' Timidly and shyly I told him my Tatar name and when he heard it he was pleasantly surprised and exclaimed, 'What a beautiful and poetic name you have!

What a fool you are to call yourself by some awful name like Roza!' Then he told me that I should not call him a Neanderthal man again and that I should beg his pardon; so, nervous and embarrassed, I squeezed out some words of apology.

He told me to remain at Alya's place, gave me a big sheet of paper and told me to make a drawing in black oil paint. I found a shoe brush in my hand and he showed me how to draw with it, rubbing it in the black oil paint which was called 'burnt bone'. For my subject he took a pillow which had been lying on the bed and said that one must portray it in all its vividness and bulkiness in space. In his magical hands the white plane was quickly obliterated, and there appeared an elusive bulk reminiscent of the familiar pillow, and around this bulk a deep space manifested itself like a halo. A kind of sacrament was taking place on this paper before our very eyes. It turned into infinite space, into an enigma. Our eyes followed it, embracing and feeling this object in space, discovering the hidden meaning in it, because apart from the pillow which he had been drawing from nature, he had also succeeded in conveying something that lay inside it. The picture was ready: it had all come to life on the paper.

Then he fastened a new sheet of paper to the plywood so that I might do one like it. Frankly, I was terrified of even taking the brush and moving it about on the paper. All I could do was to look at him with fear and nervousness while he shouted at me, 'Why are you looking at me?! Look at the paper and annihilate this flatness as quickly as possible! Why are you frightened of the paper? It isn't going to bite you! If it doesn't turn out, take a new sheet!' And overcoming my timidity and agitation I set to work on the white plane. It was more my fear that this strange, unknown man would shout at me than a fear of the white paper which made me move the brush desperately across it, and consequently my results were clumsy. There were torn white bits all over and there was no gradual transition from the white to the darker places and to the darkest black; and yet, under the artist's terrifying, uninterrupted gaze I had produced a picture. After a few repairs, smoothing down the odd torn bits, he was very satisfied with me and asked me if I wanted to study in his studio. Blushing deeply, I replied that I myself wanted to very much, but my parents would not allow me to study or go to his place; but privately I decided not to tell them about my new acquaintance and to visit him secretly. My teacher – I shall call him my teacher now, and not the stranger – then gave me his address and drew a plan of his district; and with this we parted.

The rest of the day I passed as if in a dream. I was unable to concentrate on anything and was completely brimming over with an ocean of new, hitherto unknown feelings. At home I ate silently and listened absent-mindedly to what my parents were saying, for in my thoughts I was really at Alya's place. I could hear his voice and could see his strange, enigmatic, incomprehensible appearance. That day for the first time I felt happy and quite a new person. I tried to imagine the subsequent course of my life. What it would be like was still obscure to me and my heart ached before this obscurity. My head was full of childhood memories, of my childish daydreams about a father and friend who would understand me and teach me. It seems strange to me, but, as I see now, beginning with this meeting many of my fantasies, childish dreams and desires gradually came true. Maybe I am following a path prepared for me beforehand by fate. I believe in fate. I am only resigned to it, but for some reason I always feel that there is nothing fortuitous in life: in all events past and present, in people's actions, creating love and evil, there is a Great Logic hidden from us. In it, perhaps, lies the whole meaning of our existence; but our consciousness, not seeing the whole, tries to break down all events at all times into the links of a chain and as a result there is confusion in everything. But I have gone too far and I shall resume the unconscious flow of my reminiscences, trying to find in this flow an inner logic of things.

Several days later, on a warm day in August, I set off to see my teacher. I went there not without some nervousness. Many different feelings accompanied me, the first and foremost, I think, being a vague fear of the man, a fear of finding myself alone with him. Indeed, I had been brought up by my parents to have a hatred of the opposite sex, but I don't know why they wanted me to feel like that. The second feeling I experienced was the expectation of a new world connected with my past reveries and my fantastic childhood dreams. There was the sensation of a sun shining around me as though I had found my way out of a hollow, black cave into the light. I was running out of this cave with no fear of the radiance ahead which was shining on me. I walked gaily, leaving behind the old world of my yard, my friends shelling sunflower seeds out of idleness, and all my surroundings.

My teacher lived in one of the side-streets off Sretenka in an old, three-storeyed house. I was very surprised by the similarity of our houses: I had hardly gone through the front door when I was hit by the smell of laundering with smelly, cheap soap and the stench of revolting sauerkraut soup. Two slovenly-looking women were standing by the range, one fat, the other skinny. They were quarrelling with each other. When I asked which was the artist's door, they pointed it out. Enveloped in puffs of vapour and smoke, I pulled the bell-cord and at once I could hear bells ringing, the door opened, and my teacher greeted me loudly and gaily. He was half-naked, with only khaki-coloured shorts to cover his muscular, well-proportioned body. A black, thirties-style hat was perched on his head. To my unaccustomed gaze his whole appearance seemed more than just original.

His room turned out to be very small and narrow for an artist, being only three metres long and two wide, so that there was room for only a table which stood by the window, a trestle bed covered with rugs, and opposite the trestle bed two home-made, high-backed chairs covered in bear skin. The window was large with a balcony, but the door was small and low. On the inside of the door there hung an animal skin with huge feet and claws. The table beside the window was also covered with a rug for some reason. There were rugs everywhere that space allowed. On the table stood a mug of brushes and various knick-knacks. Above the table hung an old seascape depicting a squall and fluttering rigging in the seething foam of a sinking ship with floating debris. Those were his entire furnishings. I wondered how he was able to work and, what is more, receive students at his place although on the other side of a partition his sister lived all alone in a room of twenty-five square metres. Earlier, his and his sister's rooms had formed one large room. Furthermore, suspended from the ceiling in my teacher's room and also in the communal kitchen there were kayaks which he himself had constructed according to his own designs. He even had a patent for them. How and when he began to construct these kayaks I shall tell a bit later.

My teacher seated me on the trestle bed and first treated me to some soup which he himself had made. It was a simple soup of water, potato and onion fried in vegetable oil. A wooden circle which he placed on his own or on his guest's knees served as the lunch table. During lunch he asked me about my family and my studies. He criticized me severely for calling myself by my Russian name, Roza, and he told me to drop the habit of calling myself that since I had the beautiful, poetical name of Guzel. He was sounding me out with his questions, getting to know me and measuring my possibilities to see whether it would be worthwhile bothering with me.

After lunch we got down to my lessons. Pinning a sheet of paper to some plywood, he gave me a shoe brush and a tube of black paint and told me to copy a mask of Venus which hung on the wall. I set about sketching this Venus with enormous pleasure. I liked the interesting technique, the gradations of tones and semi-tones from the light to the very darkest. But for the most part my lessons began with spheres, cones and cylinders – i.e., the simplest, it would appear, but also the most complicated lessons in the understanding of form and space – without focusing attention on the laws of perspective. At first glance this seems strange, don't you think? But it is only recently, I think, that I have begun to understand his method properly. He conceives an object, not in the usual academic sense, as something which exists in three dimensions. Instead, he sees it in an immeasurably greater number of dimensions: in four, five, and so on. If he has not yet found the key to this he has in any case come close to it, because in his teaching one could feel an outlet to infinity. He did not teach drawing by means of lines because they do not exist. What exists is our blindness, and lines are our deficiencies and defects and an inability to see the world as a whole, rather than in parts. All barriers and lines exist in our heads alone. My first lesson was very interesting and lively. Much of it I did not then understand, but I sensed what he was talking about. I drew at his place the whole day without stopping, forgetting about everything else in the world.

All the while as I drew, Vasili Yakovlevich (as my teacher was called) hummed gaily and kept running out on to the balcony, shouting something like 'Communists!' All this produced an overwhelming impression on me and I could only smile in confusion, for it was beyond my strength to object to all these pranks of his. He often joked in a very extravagant way. For example, one day he was travelling in the metro with a friend of his and opposite them sat a timid-looking man, obviously a civil servant. He was wearing a rather pretty tie. My teacher began to speak some sort of gibberish, pretending to be a foreigner – and this was at a time when foreigners were rarer in Moscow than elephants. The civil servant kept looking at him in amazement. When the train drew near a station my teacher began slowly to approach him. The civil servant shrank back, looking on in fright. Vasili Yakovlevich walked up to him calmly, took the tie off him, saying in a foreign accent, 'Sou-ve-nir!' and left the train. On another occasion – also in the metro, in winter – we were going somewhere together. He said he was starting to feel hot in the carriage and sprawling in his seat, he began, to my horror, to take off his felt boots in front of everybody. He took off his foot-cloths, too, and placed everything on the seat beside him – then ,sitting barefoot, as if nothing had happened he began with an air of indifference to whistle a pretty tune. What was it? A protest against modesty and 'long live freedom'? As I saw it, it was most likely a protest against a complex of personal inferiority and diffidence. There was a similar instance with two famous poets at the beginning of the century. It was then very fashionable to express protests of this kind. They used to go out on to the street in bright-coloured trousers and women's jackets, one yellow, the other red. They would walk down the street, embarrassing passers-by. I think one of them took his own life while still a young man, out of diffidence.

My teacher was always extravagant, not only in his behaviour, but even in his clothes. He followed the latest Western styles and loved to surprise people with his beautiful clothes; but equally he liked to startle the people around him by dressing up in what one could only call rags and tatters, and then walking along, shocking and embarrassing friends and strangers alike. For example, he purposely tore his tennis shirt, making the most intricate little holes, and then walked around in it during the summer. He made jeans for himself out of red calico flags with the result that a militiaman even stopped him and asked why he was going about looking like that and why did he use flags to make his trousers: didn't he have any other material for them? He answered the militiaman, saying that he simply had not the money to buy material for trousers so he had taken the flag off his house. I do not know how the matter ended: very likely they fined him. As a matter of fact, I remember that it was a trait of his that he always liked to make an impression on everyone around him. Whenever we walked down the street together, we were always followed by a large crowd of idlers pointing their fingers in our direction. At that time people did not easily accept reforms in clothes fashions. I remember that a girl who was acting in a film once took a room in our house. She dressed very beautifully, usually in bright-coloured clothes. Once when she wore a red coat which she herself had made, the old women in the yard, and even some who were not old, pointed at her and shouted 'Prostitute!' After the war and during the fifties clothes were on the whole sombre: dark blue, dark brown, black. If anyone dared to go out in clothes of brighter colours, he risked being spat upon and ridiculed. New styles established themselves with difficulty in Russia; perhaps it was not the right time for them. People were then tackling reconstruction on a broad front and fashion somehow fell behind, instilling into people a disregard of what they wore and at the same time implanting a crassness and wildness in the nation. Even as regards myself, I remember that when my teacher and I walked down the street followed by a huge crowd of idlers, I used to feel awkward. I was embarrassed to be walking beside him, yet at the same time I was proud of him for being unlike the others; and then I would feel ashamed of feeling ashamed and awkward in his presence.

My lessons with my teacher began not without protests on my parents' part. When my secret was discovered – and it was discovered because Vasili Yakovlevich continued to visit Alya and my parents saw us together in the yard – it became more difficult for me to go to see him. My parents were frightened of our friendship. In the first place, a suspicion had crept into their unhappy minds that I had already become his mistress. I very nearly suffered my poor Sonya's fate, namely a medical board, to which my mama wanted to subject me; but without needing any boards or delays of any kind, father called me a prostitute and my teacher a crafty villain, a libertine, an idler and a madman. In the second place, they did not consider my art studies to be work. Mama referred to my drawings contemptuously as 'sketches', saying that this all came of being idle and would lead to no good. It would be better if I went to work in a factory and acquired a skill. My father particularly attacked me, and my objections and explanations so infuriated him that he even frothed at the mouth, and once, grabbing my palette with the words, 'There have never been any artists in our family – and there never will!' hit me on the head with it, leaving my hair all different colours, while the palette itself he broke in two and threw out of the window. But gradually I managed somehow to reassure mama at least, and even to win her over a bit to my teacher's side.

Once when I was suffering from quinsy and had not gone to my lessons for a long time, my teacher unexpectedly came to visit me to find out the cause of my long absence. His arrival unbelievably upset me. I lost my head and felt enormously ashamed that he should see our wretched room and my crude parents. I was frightened of what my parents would say; but father, to my surprise, received him quite kindly and began to question him as to whether he was married, whether he had a job somewhere and how much money he earned as an artist. Then my parents invited him to eat with us and gave him noodles: that was our traditional and almost daily food. Although my father questioned him with a certain amount of mockery, telling him that this was not work, and what kind of fool would pay money for a picture, and he would not let me study painting, my teacher cited a great many examples of young artists who had been unknown at first, but went on working unceasingly until at last they became world-famous and received heaps of money for their pictures, and dressed their parents, sisters and brothers in silk. When my teacher began to talk about money, my parents' eyes lit up; and as he was leaving my father, playing the liberal, said courteously that although I should soon be working in a fur factory, I might study painting in my free time; he had nothing against that. My tearful entreaties and stubbornness had helped me, as had the presentable appearance of my teacher who had arrived in an elegant suit. By the way, his theoretical opinions fully corresponded to my parents' views on art, for in his autobiography Vasili Yakovlevich later wrote that in his opinion, 'art arose out of having nothing to do': when primitive man was himself full and he had fed his children, why should he not have sculpted amusing little men out of clay or sung in a choir? 'After all, even cranes dance and little birds sing,' he adds.

So I began going to see my teacher again and at lesson after lesson he steered me towards an understanding of art and taught me how to look and see. My lessons also included visits to museums and exhibitions. He taught me how to distinguish good works from bad, untalented ones. He enjoyed teaching me, because before him I had had no one to teach me so I had not fallen under any outside influence; my perception was fresher and unspoiled, and consequently I provided my teacher with fertile ground. I am grateful to fate for sending me such a teacher. None of his lessons and conversations was wasted: they pointed out my own way to me. On the basis of this good teacher's influence and advice, I later began to look for my own way independently, gradually moving from my teacher's method in painting to one of my own.

The life and unusual adventures of my teacher, Vasili Yakovlevich Sitnikov

Before the war my teacher had studied in the art department of the Moscow Pedagogical Institute under Professor Kardovsky and he had earned his living by working in the Surikov Art Institute. He worked there as a technician, showing slides to students. The students jokingly called him 'Vaska the Lamplighter' and the nickname persisted amongst artists. The two schools greatly differed from each other. In the institute where he studied, the students were taught how to draw every sort of form – whether it was the human figure, a plaster mask, or a pot – on ruled squares, strictly observing all the proportions, and then they went over the drawing with oil paints or water colours. When Vasili Yakovlevich took his work to show at the Surikov Institute they laughed at him openly there. He tried to work at the Surikov, imitating its method of applying free strokes of the brush on canvas, and when he took his work to show at the Pedagogical Institute, there too they made a laughing-stock of him, saying that you cannot paint that way. So he found himself caught between two fires, as it were.

Continuing to work intensely and finding himself under the influence of both schools, he gradually arrived at a method of his own, which he later taught to his pupils; by then he was openly criticizing both schools. He even succeeded in winning over a student from the Surikov Institute. He was passionately in love with her. She was German and named Irma. Sincerely convincing her that the Institute approach was incorrect and that his own was the right one, he showed her how to draw and subsequently she began to visit him and take lessons. These lessons did not last long, to be sure: the war started, she and her family were exiled somewhere, and he never managed to tell her of his love. That was his most passionate love, according to my teacher. Later on he showed me some long, ardent letters which he had written to her: some had not reached her because of her exile, but others she herself had returned to him, for while in exile she had married someone else. These letters were full of poetry and passion for her, as well as a kind of servile admiration. In any case, something unexpected happened to my teacher at this time and it affected the whole subsequent course of his life.

During my lessons I often noticed his mania for collecting objects of all kinds; in particular, he would pick up off the street jars, wire, bits of lath and plywood, beautiful bottles and even beer-bottle stoppers, explaining that he wanted to make abstract sculpture out of them. Later, a large number of cuttings from Soviet newspapers of Khrushchev and his finger appeared on his studio walls. He loved Khrushchev's index finger. Sometimes his finger would be pointing upwards, sometimes downwards – in short, it pointed in every possible direction – as if amplifying the meaning of his inspired discourse. He also collected more interesting things, for example, icons and animal skins. Now, this passion for collecting things happened to play a very fateful role in his life during the war period. When the Germans were advancing on Moscow, he and a lot of other students were sent out to dig trenches. There were German aeroplanes flying overhead at the time, dropping leaflets. Obsessed by his passion, my teacher gathered up a whole bundle of various leaflets and it lay in his home for several months amongst the other rubbish that he had collected. One day, in October or November, a friend came to see him and said mysteriously that he had picked up a German leaflet off the street and he asked if he wanted to see it, whereupon Vasili Yakovlevich replied ingenuously that he had a large number of such leaflets, and with a collector's pride he showed his bundle. The friend praised his collection and went away, and the next day some men came to see him from the Lubyanka with an order for his arrest, and they took him away together with his leaflets, without listening to his explanations.

They placed him in isolation, in a solitary confinement cell in that huge, gloomy, grey-coloured building on the Lubyanka.

They accused him not only of having the leaflets, but also of having joined an underground subversive organization, which allegedly wanted to seize the Kremlin before the Germans arrived and proclaim Vasili Yakovlevich or someone else as tsar, in order to present the Germans with the *fait accompli* of a restored monarchy in Russia. During the investigation they asked him about the other members of the group, but he denied all these senseless attacks and said that he had simply picked up the leaflets off the street for his collection. He fervently assured them that there was no group and that when he picked up the leaflets he had never dreamed that he would wind up in this sinister building. He was really very frightened of the charge of monarchism, but they did not believe him, thinking that they were faced with a cunning and hardened organizer as he would tell them nothing and denied everything. They left him in peace temporarily, meanwhile collecting information on him as he sat in his solitary cell, waiting to see what would happen, and hoping only that the whole misunderstanding would be cleared up. During his long and agonizing stay in this prison, out of whose high walls he no longer had any hope of emerging, and worn out by hunger and mental sufferings, he found an outlet in a belief in God. I do not know whether he continues to believe in Him now with such strength and humility as he did then in prison.

They did not long trouble him with interrogations. As he had not given the necessary evidence they decided to move him to Lefortovo Prison, into a cell for hardened criminals, where as a result of hunger he came down with pellagra. He was unable to walk and moved about on all fours – hunger had so worn out his body. Days passed, then a month, and a second month, and he wasn't summoned. He thought with horror that they were getting ready to finish him off. He felt wretched in his cell and he didn't even want to see his parents so much as the interrogator, in order to learn something about his fate. He decided that if they ever summoned him again he would sign any deposition whatsoever provided they would release him. He thought then of the friend who had been in his room and had seen those leaflets. It pained him to think of him. At last the door opened and the figure of the interrogator appeared, holding a statement several pages long. The interrogator told him to familiarize himself with the papers and then to sign them. My teacher was so glad of the interrogator's arrival that he did not even read the statement, but with emotion began to sign all the papers, page by page. The poor fellow! He thought that they would immediately release him as the interrogator had promised. The latter left, closing the cell door, and Vasili Yakovlevich was left with his agonizing thoughts. Fortunately or unfortunately, his testimony seemed to some higher authority rather fantastic, more like the ravings of a sick person, and a short while later he was moved to Kazan, to a prison psychiatric hospital, where he spent roughly a year.

He told me about his stay in hospital which was for lunatics. During his stay there he made a great number of drawings from life. These drawings turned out very expressive, because madmen's faces are distinguished by great character, in contrast to normal people. The movements of the soul are turned inside out on to the face and these faces are on the other side of life, as it were; and that is why it is so interesting to draw them. The attendants, huge men with ape-like faces, were distinguished by their great ferocity. They kicked the patients arbitrarily and unmercifully, attempting to strike them in the most vulnerable places, and as a result some of the prisoners became impotent. With a view to their recovery, the patients were compelled to remove their excreta in winter in forty degrees of frost. The lavatory was located outside in a small wooden shed and from time to time they had to clean it out and dispose of the excreta. The latter were frozen and you couldn't manage in the winter without a crow-bar. To what extent such work aided the patients' recovery, I do not know; but like healthy persons they showed their dissatisfaction, sometimes in a violent manner, so that afterwards the ape-like attendants would have to pacify them in the way I have described above. The wards they cleaned themselves and floor-washing was also one of their jobs. Duty rosters were set up and each one tidied up everywhere according to schedule. In order to wash oneself the following day, one had to lay in water the evening before, filling up a huge barrel. One morning someone glanced into the barrel to take some clean water, only to find excrement floating in it. This recurred day after day and they began to keep watch each morning, but they never managed to catch the offender on the spot. Then came my teacher's turn to fill up the barrel. No sooner had he filled it up and gone away, but he looked round and there was a mad Tatar getting into position over the barrel. Catching sight of Vasili Yakovlevich, he merely smiled stupidly and went on squatting there, doing what he had to do. At this point his Russian soul could bear it no longer: grabbing hold of the Tatar, he chucked him into the dirty barrel. After that the Tatar would not go near the barrel. Meanwhile my teacher's months in the Kazan psychiatric hospital came to an end and his sister assumed guardianship over him.

After such a shock and fateful blow he was for a time unable to live in Moscow and he left for his native region to regain his equilibrium a bit. He had been born in 1918 on the River Don and there he had completed navigation academy and worked as a pilot on steamers; at home in his free time he painted. As a child he had gone to Moscow periodically with his parents and in the mid-thirties he moved there for good. At first he worked on building the metro, but then he entered the Institute as I have already said. From childhood he had loved to paint. To the amusement of his parents he had painted at home even as a youth. His parents were uneducated, like mine, and because of his love of painting they considered him abnormal. 'Who needs it?' they asked. No one was going to pay even half a kopeck for it and it would be better if he chopped wood if he had nothing else to do: that would at least be useful. In the family they considered him to be a good-for-nothing; maybe that was why he had developed an inferiority complex. My parents treated my art studies in the same way, as a result of which I, too, developed a sense of diffidence although I knew that they were wrong. After leaving the ill-starred psychiatric hospital and going back home to the Don valley, my teacher slowly began to regain his equilibrium. He busied himself with his kayaks, alternating them with his art studies. Later, he moved to the capital, there to become firmly convinced of his vocation as an artist.

Distancing himself a little from his trauma, he began to enter into the main stream of post-war life in the capital. Moscow had begun to heal its wartime ravages, fattening and building itself up, studying, giving birth to a new generation, a generation with no time or beliefs, perhaps because the latter stood in the way of the new morality and consciousness. Vasili Yakovlevich once again began to work as a technician in the Surikov Institute. One of the students at the time told me later of incidents which occurred during Professor Alpatov's lectures, when my teacher was assisting the latter with his magic lantern. The lectures were on Western art and our own progressive Soviet art. 'While Soviet art increasingly blossomed and flourished,' the lecturer would say, 'Western art grew increasingly decadent, until it reached the following state of decay.' At this point my teacher would show a slide of one of Picasso's or Dali's pictures. When the students had had a look, Alpatov would say, 'Vasya, let's have the next one,' whereupon my teacher's confident voice could be heard throughout the hall:

'Wait, I'll copy this down. The picture's good: we should paint like this at home.'

Everyone would wait patiently while my teacher drew it and then the professor would continue, 'While Western art grew increasingly decadent and degenerate, Soviet art rose higher and higher, finally creating the following chef d'œuvre' – and here my teacher would show a slide of a picture by Ioganson or Serov, at the same time exclaiming, 'Shit!'

Alpatov, who was a tolerant and cultured man, and was himself perhaps depressed by the lecture he was giving, pretended not to notice his escapades or merely reprimanded him gently.

Concerning the numerous lectures he heard during his years of working in the Institute both before and after the war, my teacher remarked: 'The professors would say in their lectures one day exactly the opposite of what they had said the day before, and with the same conviction and enthusiasm; they themselves did not know what they would have to say the day after. It was enough to drive a man mad.'

But as a matter of fact my teacher did not have to work at the Institute very long, being prevented from doing so by a great scandal in which he was involved during an exhibition from the socialist countries in 1958. It was a trial balloon for assimilating foreign culture; later, under Khrushchev, these exhibitions became more frequent. My teacher was at the opening of the exhibition. There were official-looking people walking around the exhibition, loudly criticizing pictures by avant garde artists, calling them 'daubings'.

My teacher got into an argument with one of them who was looking at the pictures with an air of the greatest disgust and reviling them. After the official had listened to what my teacher had to say, he said ironically, 'Then explain this picture to us.'

Infuriated by his arrogance, my teacher replied, 'But what does an ass need art for? Why should one explain to an ass?'

The official was so surprised that he even shrank back and then my teacher saw him whispering with one of his retinue, indicating him with his eyes. The official turned out to be Minister of Culture Mikhailov, with his retinue. Following this incident Vasili Yakovlevich was dismissed from the Institute and he was left without work.

I met him three months before this episode. He himself disapproved of the exhibition, though on different grounds from Mikhailov. He found it uninteresting and told me not to go, in order not to clutter up my eyes. Sacked from the Institute, after much difficulty he got a pension through a psychiatric outpatients' clinic, in order to have some sort of official status. Otherwise he could easily have been accused of parasitism. So although this miserable pension of twelve roubles did not save him from hunger, it did save him from the arbitrariness of administrative authority. In order not to starve to death he gave private lessons, but despite the fact that he needed money, he took none from me, knowing I had none. We had an understanding that if he did not take money from me, then all the work which I did as a student in his studio could remain there permanently.

A great role in my teacher's life was played by Nina Andreyevna Stevens. Nina Andreyevna had been born in the Urals. After completing school she arrived in Moscow on a Komsomol pass to study. She entered the history department where she met an American student and shortly afterwards they got married. This was still before the war. At the end of the fifties her husband was the *Life* correspondent in Moscow. Having met the family, my teacher suggested to Nina Andreyevna the idea of collecting pictures by the 'new Russian avant garde'. At the time a second Russian artistic avant garde had begun to appear, if you count Kandinsky, Malevich, Tatlin and their contemporaries as the first.

As our great Soviet Union moves closer to the West at one moment and further away at another, so too our artistic avant garde, formed under the influence of Western art, appears and disappears. At the end of the fifties, partly under the influence of the Western art exhibitions held in Moscow, our young artists entered into a period of unusual ferment and began to work in a fairly modernist spirit, throwing off the shackles of Soviet realism. They organized underground exhibitions and had passionate discussions. As for official exhibitions, these artists could not even have dared to dream of appearing in one; but all the same, one must give Khrushchev his due for he sought reforms and established cultural ties with other countries, opening a window on to Europe so that later on someone might, in the Russian way, show his ass in the window, though now it's the face that is being shown. So, it was these new avant garde painters who were still officially unrecognized and almost persecuted, whom my teacher advised Nina Andreyevna to collect in the hope that sooner or later some of them would become famous, while in the meantime her purchases would give them support. So Nina Andreyevna formed a large collection and even exhibited it later in the USA.

She also bought pictures from my teacher and one of them even hangs in the Museum of Modern Art in New York. True, it is not the one which my teacher sold her, but the one in which he had rolled up the purchase, using an old drawing of his for the wrapper. But Nina Andreyevna bought little from him since my teacher was searching for himself then and did not always finish his pictures, abandoning them half way through. It is difficult to say to what extent he has shown his worth and whether he has found his own peculiar style. In some of his pictures, for example, in the 'Monasteries' series, he seems to be feeling his way towards his own style, or at least one of his styles. They are like Russian popular prints with gay churches and bearded peasants tearing along at full speed in their sledges. In the Russian peasant he portrays himself. But these pictures seemed to me too souvenirish, as if he had made them to order for foreigners. In due course his 'Monasteries' became very buyable. They were beautiful, of course, but very far from what my teacher could have done had he dedicated his whole life to painting.

I think my teacher understood this very well himself. I recall how once my husband and I brought some friends of ours, a young American couple, to see him. One 'Monastery' very much appealed to them and they wanted to buy it, but the price seemed too high. My teacher then told them with a smile that it was worth their while to buy it because the guests who would be visiting their home would like his 'Monastery' more than all the pictures by other artists which they had bought in Moscow, provided they never had a really good artist as a visitor. 'But where would you get one from?' my teacher added gently. 'So you may buy the picture without fear.' They bought it and were, I believe, satisfied.

So after long ordeals my teacher's life began to go smoothly. Moreover, since his house was to be rebuilt he received in place of the small room which I described earlier, two large rooms in the former French almshouse on Malaya Lubyanka, by a strange irony of fate exactly opposite that gloomy grey building where he had been taken under escort in the autumn of 1941. True, he has tightly curtained off the window looking on to that building; his flat is lit up by a window at the other end which looks on to a small, old-fashioned Moscow courtyard.

According to Vasili Yakovlevich, he is living very happily now. True, he has not become an important artist, but that in itself does not bring happiness. Perhaps he has not become an important artist precisely because he gave too much time to his students and had no energy left for himself. As a teacher, with his subtle understanding of art, his natural feeling for students and his ability to direct them on to the right path, he was perhaps my highest authority. I am very happy that I met him.

Epilogue

With the chapter devoted to my teacher I conclude my book. My meeting him marked the end of my childhood, or, in the words of Lev Tolstoy and my sister Sonya, my 'childhood and adolescence', although my 'adventures' had not yet begun. For a long time I found myself as it were between two worlds, strongly attracted by the world of the artist, but too weak to break with all the accepted notions of my parents' home; aspiring to become an artist and at times experiencing such despair and indifference that for months on end I was unable to pick up a brush; and thus I wavered until I met my future husband. I linked my destiny with his and followed him and thanks to him I was able to leave once and for all that depressing world of which I have written here. That was when my adventures really began. Sometimes I would tell my husband of my oppressive childhood memories and he advised me to write this book. I wrote it in the autumn of 1969 in our village of Akulovo outside Moscow, except for the last two chapters which I wrote in the summer of 1974 in Magadan, a town on the shore of the Sea of Okhotsk.

4 August 1974, Magadan

Letter from Siberia

My dearest, I have been meaning to write to you, but somehow I have kept putting this letter off, despite the fact that I like to write. But you yourself know what the problem is here: I am still not used to the idea that I am married. Just yesterday I told myself that it was impossible that I have got married, but now I see what a poor, naive creature I was.

How strange life is! There are such unexpected turning points, and all kinds of collisions and intricate combinations of human fates, and every person living on this earth has his own road woven out of straw and prepared for him from all these complicated combinations. But from childhood my road twisted itself out of the combinations created by my parents into quite a different direction. That is why in my patriarchal family with its philistine cosiness, I was an alien spirit, in sadness and in sorrow. My family used to say about me: it would have been better if a stone had been born instead of such a one as she. It is simply too amusing to recall how much my dear family tried to link me to my Tatar patrimony. Sometimes I offered them hope and then my family would make plans for me to marry some red-faced Tatar, but now their daughter has, against all their expectations and from an unexpected direction, made a revolution in the family, wrecked her Tatar patrimony, left home, married a godless one, a 'convict', and gone off with him to Siberia. 'What will our relatives say now?' My parents threw up their hands in great anger; my father cursed me, while mother nursed an unspoken grudge against me, sadly shaking her Tatar head. I recall my pathetic mother even now: her divine patience always touched me as she endured my father's humiliations – and, indeed, though she did not love him, she lived her whole life with him. She had been married off to an unkind husband, but she had got used to him.

Here in this Siberian village, in this hut full of holes, you sometimes stand at a frosty window, examining the patterns on the glass, and think how everything in life is a surprise, and yet it is not simply that, and I vaguely recall my dreams: everything was roads and roads and towns and in reality I was mentally preparing myself for this journey far away from my parents. I had a vague presentiment even earlier, prior to meeting Andrei, that something new would happen in my life. So I lived in sadness and sorrow, but the winds blew down from the north and brought a spirit and he carried me off beyond great rivers to the great taiga and a village so tiny that it barely sticks up out of the earth; and he took my heart and made me his wife.

So, we are living here – in anxiety, labour and gladness. Andrei is now cleaning the cowshed from ten in the morning to four. I, too, have work to do and rather a lot of it: I have to get up before him, heat the stove and make breakfast. Our food is as follows: for breakfast, mashed potatoes; for lunch, fried potatoes; for supper, potatoes, merely boiled. They give us one litre of milk a day which we use as we please. Sometimes the local inhabitants give us an onion out of the goodness of their hearts. I go out for the water and it is a very long way to go, some three hundred metres. I have learned how to launder under the conditions here. It is interesting that as a child my idea of a village was associated with peasant women rinsing their laundry in an ice-hole and now this association has been confirmed. Here only things like washing and rinsing, especially in freezing weather, are considered difficult.

Congratulate me on starting to work and really rather productively. For example, I have made two very good portraits: one of Andriusha, the other, a self-portrait with a frosty window as background. Andrei likes his portrait very much. He can never see enough of it and praises it highly, saying that it has refinement and elongation in the style of El Greco. Well, I don't know why he's such a flatterer. I think women like this in him most of all and he is going to melt the whole of Siberia with his flattery, and the little spring brooks will begin to flow unexpectedly, flowers will bloom, and an imaginary spring will begin outside our door and shower praises on Andriusha, and his nice cows with their big tits, for which he shows greater preference than mine, will come in an entire herd to graze in our yard.

Fairly often, drunk peasant men and women drop in on us to chat in the evenings. They get drunk on home-brewed beer which they drink by the litre here: there is nothing else to do. So they come to visit to have a stare at us. It is very interesting when they find themselves on our doorstep. They stand there rooted to the spot, goggle stupidly with their red eyes, scratch the backs of their heads, and only later sit down on the doorstep and slowly loosen their tongues, shouting each word at the top of their voice. They don't notice this themselves, but privately we find it amusing. They look at my paintings and praise them, although they have absolutely no idea that these are paintings and not photographs. They do not even know the word 'painting'. They commission me to do 'portraits', but we make it a condition that they must give us five roubles plus five roubles' worth of meat; they hesitate, but we would like to get money for meat and sugar. In the meantime one has to make both ends meet somehow.

There are very few men in this village, but there are heaps of children in every hut and all of them different, bearing no resemblance to each other. The inhabitants have lived here for a very long time, having moved from one hole to another, from Byelorussia to Western Siberia. Some of the men were killed in the war, while others have left, so the women marry exiles. The latter stay their term, working on a collective farm and living in a warm place and with a woman besides and lard, too. What's so bad about that? They have home-brewed beer in place of tea and they gulp down home-brewed vodka as if it were soup. They give a woman a lot of children and then go off wherever they like. But under Stalin anyone who was sound and healthy went through all the local women he could find as our friend, the artist Weisberg, says. Large numbers of exiles were sent here and on top of that a tremendous lot of taxes were collected from the inhabitants, so life was very hard for the women, the children had different fathers and there was also much fatherlessness. But they got used to this and whenever an exile arrives they entice him to live with them: life is easier with a man, they have large holdings to look after, firewood has to be laid in for the winter, and it makes life jollier. Sometimes you will see a quite young fellow living with an old woman, but what more does he need? He's got meat and home-brewed beer, and a warm roof over his head, and somehow after a drinking bout he gets to know the old woman. In this village now there are four exiles, not counting Andriusha, and they have all settled down with old women in this way. They come to see us sometimes and each one starts shouting at the top of his voice about his old woman: she's this and she's that, she wouldn't let me drink, she hid the home brew, I'm going to give her a fright. And yesterday one hopeless drunkard told us how he had ripped up her dress with his teeth and beat her with a poker: 'Let me drink,' he said; 'if you don't, I'll burn the hut down, so there!' This hopeless drunkard arrived with some pork under his jacket. He had brought it to sell to us cheap, two kilograms for a rouble and a half, so that he could get drunk quickly. Inwardly rejoicing, though outwardly preserving our impenetrability, we naturally accepted the pork under his stern instructions not to tell his old woman; we needed it badly for as a matter of fact we had not had meat almost from the time we left Moscow.

We had still not registered our marriage officially so we travelled for this purpose to the district capital eighteen kilometres away. We left for there in the middle of the day so consequently we were late and had to turn the horse around and come back home, this time in the dark. We returned home slowly; there were still two villages ahead of us and it was freezing cold. So we went at an unhurried jog-trot straight into the night, urging our weary Sikukha homewards – and all round was the taiga, a bit frightening, the trees with their dark branches reminding me of monsters' paws, and the frosty, ringing silence. It was strange and marvellous to me, and wonderful, too, to see the heavenly dome strewn with stars. The stars here are so big and bright that they make you forget about the taiga, your marriage and unhappy Andrei; you forget about the road and the distance and poor Sikukha, and you become a part of all these boundless stars and join the chorus of cosmic melody. Now, as I write this, I am thinking to myself: I'm like Sonya, my silly sister; everything is stars, stars with her, too. . . . But when we finally dragged ourselves up to our little hut on its chicken legs I had to come down out of the heavenly dome and go into our little hut and continue our life of sin until we could find a convenient time for another trip to Krivosheino. So ended our long poetic journey on a 'dashing steed' with the starry cosmic melody and the piercing shouts with which Andriusha filled the taiga and its ringing silence as he cleaved the frosty air with his lash, desperately whipping our weary Sikukha.

We have lived in sin for more than a month, but we haven't gone off there a second time, although it has long been rumoured in our village that I am not his 'lawful' wife and that I have been living here for some time but am still not registered. Perhaps we shall go off in a day or two when they have sent some felt boots from home. Mine have quite fallen to pieces: when you walk in water, they become sopping wet, because there are holes in the heels. I am not in the least embarrassed about living in sin, for what good came of my abiding in a state of stupid virginity, of no use to anyone? I wonder what my mother would say if she heard me say that? My father would cut off my head immediately; but it doesn't matter. I don't want to go back to Moscow, although we are suffering quite a few deprivations here; for example, the hut is full of holes, with cracks everywhere, and when we heat the stove, the heat doesn't last long and it's never really very warm. I don't know how Andrei will live when I go: he'll come back from work and the stove will be cold. He'll have to heat it and cook his own dinner and he won't be able to rest and it's so far to go for water. We have no sugar; our larder is almost empty. Fortunately, for the time being we still have some vegetable oil and millet groats, but even that will come to an end soon and I don't know whether they will bring provisions for him on his own; after all, the other exiles have settled in rather well, temporarily marrying old women. For the present we are doing without sugar for life is sweet for us even without it, but suddenly our love will cool down, and then our stove won't warm up our hearts, and the missing sugar will have done its part, and we shall become cachectic corpse-bodies.

Your letter has arrived and it has made us very worried by its confusion. The bear has disappeared which has terribly grieved Andriusha. You are ill and plan to go to hospital: it's your heart, isn't it? What a nuisance! All in all, Andriusha is greatly grieved by the whole business. You should have tried to keep well, my dear, my darling; what a hard time you are having with your heart and throat, and then there are the children.

Well, get better soon and look after yourself, to stay attractive. I kiss you, you who are so near and dear to our hearts.

Your Guzel

25 November 1965, Guryevka.

Meeting in the prison camp

In the summer of 1971 I received a letter from the camp. It was my husband writing that our meeting had been set for the winter and that they had given us three whole days! So, with uneasy feelings I immediately began to get ready, in keeping with the Russian proverb: 'Prepare your sleigh in the summer and your cart in the winter.' Now I was presented with an opportunity to fulfil this adage, because in Russia it is never possible to get what you need straight away.

Now it is winter, and after a twelve-hour flight I am in Magadan, in a small, dirty airport. My Andrei is languishing quite near me now, for Talaya settlement where the camp is located is only 250 kilometres to the north. Magadan appeared to me grey, cheerless and foggy; only the mountains surrounding the town seemed beautiful and majestic. The Sea of Okhotsk was frozen and there was a strong, gusty wind blowing.

The next day I left for Talaya by the only bus. In front of me sat a tall, thick-set man in a dark coat with procurator's insignia on his cuffs. He kept exchanging glances with a young couple and often turned in my direction, looking at me significantly. Finally he asked if I was not going to see my husband. So I reached Talaya towards evening along with the procurator.

In his letter my husband had given me the address of a girl with whom I might stay. I walked at random, with huge bundles in my hands and a rucksack on my back, until I saw a wrinkled old woman – before I saw her I had encountered only soldiers and I had decided not to ask the way of them – and the old woman conducted me uphill, past a by-street with tiny houses and faceless, concrete three-storey buildings. I found it unbearably difficult to carry my load, but the old woman rushed ahead with amazing speed and at last we reached a hostel standing on a hill, This was a long, thin, white structure, which people of working-class appearance were continually entering and leaving. A long corridor ran along the inside and there were rooms on either side.

Lena greeted me in a friendly way. The room contained only two iron beds, a small table and in the corner a narrow clothes cupboard; there was also just enough room for two chairs. A girl of about eight was sitting on a bed, thumbing a dog-eared book. She turned out to be Lena's younger sister; their mother was dead. Lena was twenty-six and unmarried, although she struck me as a pretty blonde. In this room there also lived another young unmarried woman, Masha, with her own daughter who was the same age as Lena's sister. The four of them slept on the two narrow beds.

An hour later a drunk man, a friend of Masha's, arrived and before everyone's eyes began to make advances to her. The little girls who were serious beyond their years and understood what was happening moved into a corner of the bed and pretended not to notice anything as they played with their dolls. Now and then they stole a peek at the couple and whispered together. Then Lena's friend arrived, sober on this occasion. It was unbearably cramped in this room of ten square metres and it was painful to look at the miserable girls and the unfortunate women.

The next day I was at the camp and learned that our meeting would be arranged only in the evening. I decided to have a look at the settlement and the famous Talaya spa which was situated two kilometres from the camp. It was hard to believe that the two could be compatible, but there was a mineral spring here and they had decided to construct a northern spa. They had begun with the camp so that the prisoners could then construct the spa. Many of the camp authorities' wives were employed in the spa and the two girls with whom I was staying also worked there as waitresses, feeding their children by bringing home left-over soup and meat. They also contrived to filch sugar and baked goods: in the cupboard beneath the clothes lay heaps of sugar taken from the spa.

I was astonished by the contrast between the buildings of the spa which resembled pompous palaces with columns, grottoes, fountains and a large pool, and the wretched houses of the settlement, and the terrible broken roads strewn with pieces of the local rock.

Looking down from my hostel window I could see an area enclosed by a high fence and barbed wire: this was the woodworking centre where the prisoners worked. A long column was on its way there from the camp, with two soldiers with dogs front and behind. The prisoners walked along downcast in great quilted jackets and tarpaulin boots. The temperature was —20°C, and as a matter of fact it can go as low as —60°C. In my agitation I ran out of the house and began to wave to the prisoners with my long scarf. Some of them saw me and the last one replied with a wave of the hand. For a minute I thought it was Andrei although I knew that he did not have to do such heavy work, having become an invalid while in prison, following an attack of meningitis. At this point one of the soldier escorts started to drive the prisoner on, poking him in the back with his rifle muzzle, and the dogs began to bark loudly. Later I found out that of course this was not Andrei. But I think the prisoners must have liked seeing a woman waving to them from above. Many of them knew that Andrei was expecting his wife to visit him and they described me to him, so he learned of my arrival.

Dusk set in and I got ready in a state of great agitation. For me this longed-for meeting seemed like a first encounter in youth; and in fact we had been away from each other for almost a year and a half. How would he greet me? Would there not be some feeling of alienation between us? After all, when you live together the development of character is not so noticeable as it is in separation; and it was with such apprehensions that I found myself beside the prison camp wall.

First I was admitted to the room of the officer of the day. My passport was taken and checked to see if our marriage had been noted in it; then they examined all the contents of my rucksacks and travelling bag. They even cut the chocolate into pieces in case there was some sort of political manifesto or letters from friends inside it. They also looked to see if I was carrying a tape recorder or a camera. What if people outside the camp should see a photograph of my husband who had already lost twenty kilograms and was nothing but skin and bones? Then they noticed a tiny bottle of brandy and put it aside with the word, 'Unauthorized!' And I had so hoped that we would be able to celebrate the arrival of the New Year with this symbolic portion of brandy.

Then they led me down a corridor, through a door which opened and shut automatically, and then down another little corridor into a narrow room with two neatly covered iron beds, a table and two chairs. It resembled my girls' room in the hostel, or a room in some country hotel, the only difference being that here the small window was barred. I paid for the room, too, like in a hotel.

My husband was not in the room. Instead, there was a fairly old woman waiting for me, all wizened, with a wicked expression on her face. The officer who had escorted me went away and she fell headlong upon me like a panther and began to frisk me, requesting me to undress voluntarily: time wouldn't wait, she said, and it was in my own interest to see my husband as soon as possible. I refused to do it whereupon she simply felt me and all the seams in my clothes. Grabbing my comb unceremoniously, she jerked it through my hair, thinking that there might be something unauthorized hidden even there. It was like a nightmare: I protested feebly like a sleep-walker, but she ran the comb through my hair again, satisfying herself that there was nothing of interest to her there. I told her that I would make a complaint and in reply she snapped that she was afraid of no one; she had been here for thirty years, knew all the procedures and obeyed all the rules. She wanted to take away my penholder and even my make-up pencil, but I stubbornly refused to give them to her.

She left at last, and in a temper and all in tears, and anxious because Andrei was about to appear, I began to put on my pretty French peignoir, lit a candle, spread our favourite, although by now threadbare, red tablecloth, which I had brought from home – and suddenly the door opened and my husband's slight figure appeared, or rather his shadow, so emaciated was he, wearing an impossible white cap like

Petrushka and grey overalls with a number sewn on. We threw ourselves at each other and we felt that we had never been separated, although his face, which was very emaciated and covered in pimples owing to a lack of vitamins, brought us back to reality.

Those three days were like a dream to us. We did not want to think how quickly they would pass. I tried to fatten Andrei up a bit; I had brought a lot of delicious things from Moscow and I cooked right in the room on an electric stove, but he was almost unable to eat. After our very first supper he became so ill that the next day we had to send for the camp doctor who gave him an injection. I shall say something more about this woman doctor later.

I was so excited: I felt that these days would be insufficient to relate all my news. The important things I tried to write down on paper or say under the covers, because we knew that microphones had been placed in the room. Andrei also wrote a long letter to his Dutch friend, Karel van het Reve, in which he described how he had been taken, a sick man, all the way across Siberia; I was to smuggle this letter out and forward it to Holland.

When we parted I left Andrei some warm underwear and I wanted to give him some shorts into the elastic of which I had sewn several ten-rouble notes for him to spend illegally in camp, buying provisions from men who had been able to bring them in secretly from outside; but Andrei would not take the shorts, saying that the money would certainly be found and confiscated during the search following our meeting.

They took Andrei away and suddenly into the room came an officer and two women. One was the old woman who had already searched me: she worked here as a censor and checked the prisoners' letters. The other, a younger woman, was the doctor who had come to examine Andrei; she was wearing a white smock and gynaecological gloves. The officer said that these women would quickly look my things over and immediately let me go, after which he went out leaving the three of us. They began again efficiently to feel every seam and their joy knew no bounds when they discovered the money sewn into the shorts.

The old one, casting her eyes maliciously at me the whole time, said to her colleague, 'I wouldn't be sorry even to kill such people!' and continued, 'Here we are, working, and we don't even see the light of day. We're of use to the state, but all you do is spread slander. You're anti-Soviets! They didn't give him enough, that husband of yours. I'd let him rot here!' I kept silent, clenching my teeth, but later on I couldn't contain myself and I called her an old fascist.

After they had examined my things, they came over to me and asked me to undress. I refused: I wasn't a prisoner yet, to have to undress for a search. The woman in rubber gloves was all ready for it. I started to shout at them, demanding the procurator. Then, laughing insolently, they sat down at the table at which my husband and I had had breakfast that morning and one of them said to the other, 'I feel like having some tea.' It was interesting that even while having tea the doctor sat in her gynaecological gloves the whole time, even holding a piece of sugar in them.

Two hours passed like that. I repeated over and over again: keep me as long as you want, but I won't let you search me; I'll talk only to the procurator. Two more hours passed and I began to feel hungry. There were many delicious things left over from our meeting, because prisoners have no right to take anything with them, so I had a bite to eat while they watched me enviously: they were drinking tea with some kind of dry rusks. Then I took a little nap which so infuriated them that they began to quarrel. 'My work is already finished, my son is home from school, and I'm still not back!' said the doctor in exasperation.

At this point I wanted to go out to relieve myself, but they would not release me; instead they fetched a bucket, placed it in the middle of the room and said, 'We're not men: you can do it in front of us without feeling embarrassed.' I prayed to all the saints that Andrei's papers would not fall out during this operation for I had concealed them deeply; but I relieved myself safely under the intense gaze of two pairs of eyes. They had calmed down a bit, I think. One of them left the room and reappeared two minutes later with the procurator of Magadan Province, the very same one with whom I had travelled in the bus, although hitherto they kept saying that there was no procurator here.

The procurator greeted me like an old friend, listened attentively and ordered them to let me go, although I would have to see the camp commandant. When I went off to see him, in the corridor I ran into the same young couple that had travelled with me in the bus. Seeing me, they disappeared into one of the rooms. I learned later that some employees of the KGB had come here for the duration of my meeting with Andrei; perhaps it was precisely these two.

The commandant got up from behind his desk and came over to meet me with a smile. This surprised me: usually a commandant sits at his desk taking in the visitor with a cold, casual glance, then utters a strained greeting and a regular interrogation begins. But he asked me humanely how the meeting had gone and I mentioned the six-hour search. Then he asked why men's shorts with money sewn into them had been found amongst my things. I replied in a very confident tone, 'And why do you think that these shorts were meant for my husband? After all, they weren't found on him. They're my shorts and the money was sewn into them so I wouldn't lose it during my trip.' I don't think he believed me, but he did not touch on this again. Afterwards my husband lodged some complaints and obliged them to return the money.

The commandant asked whether I knew Solzhenitsyn, and why did he write only terrible things, and show everything in the worst light? Don't we have any bright sides? I asked whether he had read Solzhenitsyn's books.

'I've only read *One Day in the Life of Ivan Denisovich*, which is a very interesting story.'

'So how can you say that he describes only terrible things, if you've read only one story?'

'I have read criticisms in the newspapers and I have no reason not to believe them.'

With this, our discussion of Solzhenitsyn came to an end. The commandant got up, pulled a fountain pen out of his pocket and said that it was Korean and that he was giving it to me. His expression was rather one of sympathy and with the same affable smile he escorted me to the door. Maybe he was being cunning with me, fearing that I might make complaints to Moscow; maybe he really sympathized with me. I had the impression that his work was beginning to oppress him and he was soon removed from this post.

Free at last! It was already dark outside. I went down the hill along a moonlit road. I walked along in an agitated state and suddenly, after walking some three hundred metres, I turned round instinctively and went back to the camp. I walked up to headquarters, looked through the bright window and saw my Andrei standing and arguing about something with the officer of the day. I began pounding on the window and shouting through the casement that everything was all right, that they had detained me for six hours, but now everything was well: 'Take care of yourself, and wear the hat I've brought you.' Andrei was indescribably glad to see me. He had been terribly worried about me, but now he calmed down. We kept on saying 'good-bye' excitedly through the window until the officer rudely cut short our cries, slamming the casement and drawing the curtain.

Now I went back to the settlement calmly, but ahead of me I still had Magadan and Moscow. I sent Andrei's letter on to Holland with friends, and it is still kept by Karel van het Reve in a strong-box.

November 1976, Utrecht
(five years after the events described)

Guzel Amalrik